MODERN TIMES

The Making of the Welfare State

R. J. Cootes MA

LONGMAN

LONGMAN GROUP LIMITED
London
*Associated companies, branches and representatives
throughout the world*

© Longman Group Ltd. 1966

First published 1966
Seventh impression 1977
ISBN 0 582 20428 3

*Printed in Hong Kong by
Sheck Wah Tong Printing Press Ltd*

Acknowledgements

For permission to reproduce photographs we are grateful to the following: *Daily
Mirror*—page 88; Greater London Council—page 25; London Express News and
Feature Services—page 83; National Portrait Gallery—pages 4 and 12; *Northern
Echo*—pages 69 and 124; *Punch*—pages 40, 49, 94, 108, 116 and 127; *The Times*—
page 21; Vandyk—page 67; York Corporation (through the City Engineer and
Planning Officer)—page 71. All others are by courtesy of the Radio Times Hulton
Picture Library.

Unemployment Insurance and Assistance	Health Insurance	Other schemes

HC|FE

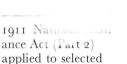

Unemployment Insurance and Assistance	Health Insurance	Other schemes
1911 National Insurance Act (Part 2) applied to selected trades only	1911 ... surance Act (Part 1) applied to lower-paid workers	... Compensation extended to most occupations
1920 Unemployment Insurance extended to most workers		1923 Workmen's Compensation further extended
1921 Dependants' Allowances. 'Extended benefits' allowed		
1931 'Means test' applied to Public Assistance payments		
1934 Insurance and Assistance separated— the latter made the responsibility of the Unemployment Assistance Board		
1946 National Insurance Act applied to all citizens of working age. Benefits for 'interruption of earnings' due to sickness, unemployment or old age	1946 National Health Service— free to all	1945 Family Allowances Act
		1946 Industrial Injuries Act (Workmen's Compensation replaced by new scheme)
1966 Wage-related Short-term Benefits		1971 Family Income Supplements
1975 Earnings Related Benefits		

Titles in this series

Contents

Introduction

The meaning of the Welfare State

Early in July 1948 the *Daily Mail* told its readers: 'On Monday morning you will wake in a new Britain, in a State which "takes over" its citizens six months before they are born, providing care and free services for their birth, for their early years, their schooling, sickness, workless days, widowhood and retirement. All this, with free doctoring, dentistry and medicine—free bath-chairs, too, if needed—for 4*s*. 11*d*. out of your weekly pay packet. You begin paying next Friday.' The great day in question was 'vesting day' of the Welfare State, 5 July, when most of the social services of modern Britain came into operation.

Things like this do not happen suddenly out of the blue. The British Welfare State was won after a long struggle going back well into the last century. In this book you will be able to trace that struggle, stage by stage. It was fought by ordinary people—your fathers and grandfathers among them—to win financial security in times of hardship and a fair share of the benefits of civilisation, which had so long been beyond their reach. The story of the Welfare State shows that history is not always about 'battles and great men' and that the greatest achievements of mankind can be the least dramatic.

Perhaps when we know more about the way people lived in the days before the Welfare State, we will really appreciate how lucky we are to be living in the second half of the twentieth century.

1 'Self-Help'

Have you ever wondered what sort of life you would have had if you had been born a century earlier—in the reign of Victoria, 1837–1901 ? We have all read stories of great country houses, where some people lived a life of leisure with countless servants and everything they wanted; but what of the ordinary working people, who were the vast majority? In an age when Britain was the most powerful country in the world, with an empire which stretched across the globe, the greatest navy, and the most advanced industries, there existed in this country, amid riches and plenty for the few, millions of people living out their lives in misery and squalor.

Rich and poor

Benjamin Disraeli, who later became an outstanding Prime Minister, wrote a book in 1845 in which he described the rich and poor as Two Nations '. . . between whom there is no sympathy; who are as ignorant of each other's habits, thoughts and feelings as if they were dwellers in different zones, or inhabitants of different planets; who are formed by different breeding; are fed by a different food, are ordered by different manners, and are not governed by the same laws'.

In the previous year, a German reformer, Friedrich Engels, gave this vivid account of early Victorian town life: 'A horde of ragged women and children swarm about, as filthy as the swine that thrive on the garbage heaps and in the puddles . . . The race that lives in these ruinous cottages behind broken windows . . . or in dark wet cellars in measureless stench and filth . . . must really have reached the lowest stage of humanity.' Engels was not exaggerating. In Manchester at this time over sixty babies out of every hundred born died before the age of five. In Liverpool, one family in five lived in a damp, dark cellar. Cholera and other killing diseases raged in the towns—encouraged by the appalling lack of sanitation.

At the other extreme, some rich, aristocratic families lived a life of luxury and idleness. A constant round of balls and parties, hunting and shooting, cards and billiards, amateur theatricals and music-making was carried on in great mansions or pleasantly-situated houses. These often stood in beautiful parks, and employed scores of butlers, cooks, gardeners and servants of all kinds. Mrs Stanhope, in Anthony Trollope's novel *Barchester Towers*, was far from being one of the aristocracy, yet she was typical of a 'woman of leisure' of this period: 'Her dress was always perfect; she never dressed but once in a day, and never appeared till between three and four; but when she did appear, she appeared at her best . . . her ornaments were costly, rare and such as could not fail to attract notice . . . But when we have said that Mrs Stanhope knew how to dress . . . we have said all. Other purpose in life she had none.'

As you can see, the gulf between the 'Two Nations' was very great. While the woman of leisure frittered away her time, secure from the anxieties of the outside world, a woman of the labouring class worked a long day in a factory or on the land for a few shillings a week. Babies were often taken into factories and put on the floor by the machines while their mothers worked. Children took full-time jobs as young as six or seven to help make ends meet. Yet the most likely reward for this life of toil was poverty and an early grave.

'Self-Help'

Most of the well-to-do Victorians were ignorant of the way working people really lived. Many shut their eyes to the problems and simply said it was up to the poor to help themselves. They genuinely believed that it made a man spineless if he was given a helping hand—that he would always want to lean on someone else rather than stand on his own feet. This attitude was summed up by Samuel Smiles in a book called *Self-Help* (1859). He said hard work was the answer to poverty, for 'they who are the most persistent, and work in the truest spirit, will invariably be the most successful'. In a later book,

Samuel Smiles—populariser of self-help

called simply *Thrift* (by which he meant a careful use of money, putting some by for when it was needed), he said: 'How much of human happiness depends on the spending of the penny well . . . a penny saved is the seed of pounds saved.'

It was all very well for Samuel Smiles, along with prosperous industrialists and business men, to preach the people smug sermons about the virtue of being a self-made man. In fact, it took ability, ambition and a large slice of luck for an unskilled labourer, with no education, to improve his position in the world. How could the working class save money when their wages were often so low that they could not manage in a normal week? Needless to say, if these families struggled under normal conditions you can imagine how hard life would be for them if the family income was suddenly reduced by sickness, unemployment, old age or death. They could not afford to 'save for a rainy day', so they were totally unprepared for such a calamity. If the father died, or was out of work for a long period, his wife had to carry on somehow without his wages. 'Self-help' sounded a good idea in theory, but it could not provide an answer to problems like these.

The better paid, more highly skilled workers could help themselves. They could afford weekly subscriptions to a Friendly Society or a trade union, in return for which they received money benefits in time of need. There were well over a million members of Friendly Societies by the mid-nineteenth century. For their weekly payments, members usually got an allowance during sickness, a pension in old age and a sum of money at death to help with the funeral expenses. Most of these societies were small, local organisations, but there were some large, national ones, like the 'Hearts of Oak', established in 1841. Ordinary labourers were not admitted, however; only those earning above a certain wage were eligible.

Many trade unions provided benefits for members, in the same way as the Friendly Societies, although these were secondary to their main purpose of trying to obtain improvements in wages and conditions of work. In the rules of the Amalgamated Society of Engineers, established in 1851, it stated that one of the tasks of the union was 'to promote the general and material welfare of its members, to assist them when out of work or in distressed circumstances, to support them in case of sickness, accident or superannuation (old age), and loss of tools by fire, to provide for their burial and the burial of their wives'.

Thus the better paid workers had something to fall back on in time of hardship. However, those who either had no trade union or could not afford any weekly payments had to manage as best they could if they came upon hard times. This could mean no fuel in winter and insufficient food and clothing. Although a good deal of charity was given by the rich to the poor, a large number of people suffered unnoticed, through no fault of their own.

Looking at this state of affairs a century later, we naturally ask, 'Why didn't the government do something about it?'

Victorian charity—a soup kitchen in the East End of London, 1867

Nowadays we expect our rulers to prevent things like this happening. However, in the mid-nineteenth century, governments did not think it was their duty to provide schemes of welfare and assistance for people who suffered hardship. They believed that as long as they kept the peace and looked after British interests at home and abroad, organised the nation's finances and corrected only the most glaring abuses in national life that, for the rest, the people would be able to look after their own affairs. By taking this view they were merely reflecting the spirit of the age. Not until the end of the century was this attitude seriously challenged and shown to be somewhat optimistic.

The Poor Law

Victorian governments did, however, allow one important exception to the general principle of self-help. A Poor Law Act of 1834 had set up a system of workhouses for the totally destitute. If people found themselves jobless, homeless, sick, or faced with starvation, there was always the workhouse to fall back on if no one else could help. It was a last resort, and not a pleasant one at that. In order to encourage people to help themselves, and to discourage idlers from trying to get free board and lodging, life in a workhouse was made less com-

Men breaking stones in a labour yard

fortable than that of the lowest class of labourer. The occupants were set to work, in return for which they received the bare minimum of food and some kind of bed. Discipline was strict: families were separated, complete silence observed at meals, visiting and visitors prohibited, and smoking and beer-drinking not allowed. It goes without saying that these places were hated and feared by the poor. Many preferred to face starvation rather than go into the workhouse.

Workhouses were paid for out of the parish rates, and the ratepayers (householders) elected local Boards of Guardians to run them. Guardians were ratepayers themselves, so they had an interest in keeping down the running costs of the workhouse. This usually meant that the food provided was just about enough to keep body and soul together. In *Oliver Twist*, the famous novel about an orphan who was born and reared in a workhouse, Charles Dickens strongly attacked the whole system. Poor Oliver had to exist on a diet of gruel (a thin food made by boiling oatmeal in water). Of this, 'each boy had one porringer, and no more—except on occasions of great public rejoicing, when he had two ounces and a quarter of bread besides. The bowls never wanted washing. The boys polished them with their spoons till they shone again . . .'

Victorian workhouses had a character of their own, but they were not a new idea. The first national system of poor relief dates back to the reign of the first Elizabeth, 1558–1603. 'The Acte for the Releife of the Poore' (1598) made each parish raise local taxes, or rates, for helping its poor, handicapped and destitute people. From these rates, 'Houses of Correction' were built for 'rogues and idlers', while the unemployed poor were given 'a convenient stock of materials' upon which they could work at home.

An important new departure, called the 'Speenhamland system', began in 1795. Because of rising prices during the French wars, farm labourers' wages had become insufficient for even the bare necessities of life. In Berkshire, the magistrates, meeting in the parish of Speen, decided to make labourers' wages up to a basic minimum out of the local rates. The amount of relief given in each case varied according to the price of bread and the number of children in the family. This allowance system was soon adopted throughout southern England. Unfortunately, farmers took advantage of it to refuse necessary increases in wages—knowing their workers could get relief from the parish. Thus, while the rates went up alarmingly, the poor labourers were humiliated by receiving part of their income in the form of parish charity.

The Poor Law Amendment Act (1834) replaced the Speenhamland system. It discouraged the able-bodied poor from applying for relief by making them enter a workhouse to get it, although the aged and sick could stay in their homes. However, in practice, it was usually cheaper and more convenient for the Guardians to herd everyone together under one roof. In some places the sick were looked after by the insane in filthy workhouse infirmaries. Orphans mixed with hardened criminals, destitute mothers with prostitutes; while those who had lived respectable lives but were forced to enter the workhouse in old age were mixed with those whose poverty was due to drunkenness and vice.

Being a pauper was now a bigger disgrace than ever before. As Disraeli said, the 1834 Act 'announced to the world that in England poverty is a crime'. Not surprisingly, the numbers on poor relief dropped sharply after 1834. The authorities were delighted, for they intended the workhouses to be a deterrent. Nevertheless, conditions were gradually improved during the nineteenth century. Workhouse schools were intro-

Marylebone workhouse in west London. A new ward for the homeless poor, 1867

duced to help fit children for an independent life. Care of the sick was made more humane, although Guardians were not permitted to supply such 'expensive' medicine as cod liver oil until 1864. By the 1880s, however, the sick could be admitted to poor law hospitals without being classed as paupers.

The main features of the Victorian poor law remained until well into the twentieth century. However, long before this, there was increasing pressure on the Government, from many quarters, for them to adopt a more kindly attitude towards helping the needy. It was clearly unfair to treat all paupers alike. People began to distinguish between the idlers and the 'deserving poor', and urged the Government to help the latter. After all, thrift and hard work were not always enough to keep a family out of poverty. A year's bad luck could destroy the careful management of a lifetime. Nevertheless, Parliament was slow to act.

2 Parliament and Social Reform

In the nineteenth century, the Government was not expected to give the 'underdog' a helping hand. If people failed to make ends meet, for any reason whatever, it was their own business. Government interference in family life was frowned upon—even though many families, forced by poverty to enter a workhouse, were broken up for ever. W. E. Gladstone, four times Prime Minister, summed up this attitude: 'Let the government labour to its uttermost . . . (the answer to) the question whether the English father is to be the father of a happy family and the centre of a united home . . . must depend on himself.' This was small comfort to a family whose father was out of work, crippled or even dead!

However, before we condemn the Victorians for their indifference to the sufferings of the poor, we should consider another, more positive, aspect of government. Although Parliament ignored individual hardship, it was willing to improve the dreadful working and living conditions in the new industrial towns. Things like laying drains, paving, cleansing and lighting the streets, and protecting women and children in the factories and mines, were best dealt with on a large scale by the Government rather than by private individuals all going their separate ways. A great deal was achieved in this direction—so much, in fact, that Victoria's reign is often called an 'age of reform'.

Factories and mines

The early factories, most of them making textile goods, were established in great numbers from the latter part of the eighteenth century onwards. Hundreds, or even thousands, of workers were brought together under one roof, usually in foul, stuffy conditions amid the whirr of machinery. In their haste to make big profits, most of the factory owners ignored the needs of their workers. Hours were long and wages low, so it was necessary for the whole family to work. Children of six or seven worked the same hours as adults—anything up to sixteen a day! Dragged from their beds in the early hours of the morning, they often had to be beaten to keep them awake at their work. Sometimes exhausted children fell into the machines or slept on the roadside on their way home, to be rescued by their parents.

Children working in a textile factory in the 1840s

The plight of these factory children soon attracted the attention of reformers. Their earliest achievements—the Acts of 1802 and 1819—which restricted children's hours of work, were largely ignored by the factory owners. Not until 1833 was the first really effective Factory Act passed. It barred all children under nine from textile factories and limited the hours of older children to forty-eight a week for those under

Anthony Ashley Cooper, seventh Earl of Shaftesbury

thirteen and sixty-nine for 'young persons' of thirteen to eighteen. For the first time, paid inspectors were appointed to see that the law was observed. In addition, it was laid down that every factory child was to receive two hours' schooling a day, but this was difficult to enforce and thus often ignored.

The great importance of the 1833 Act was that it established the principle of State intervention between employers and workers to control hours and working conditions. It was the first real success for a small group of energetic reformers—the most outstanding being Anthony Ashley Cooper (1801–85), later Lord Shaftesbury, who devoted all his life and his money to social reform. Lord Ashley was the force behind the Government's appointment of a Royal Commission on Children's Employment in 1840. Two years later, the Commission reported on the condition of underground workers in the mines. The public was horrified to learn that young girls, naked to the waist, were chained to coal tubs which they dragged, on all fours, along underground passages for twelve or more hours a day! A Mines Act (1842) prohibited the employment of women and girls underground, and a minimum age of ten was fixed for the employment of boys.

The Royal Commission reported on other industries in the following year, and its findings led to another important Factory Act in 1844. It reduced women's hours by including

Woman and child drawing coal in a mine, 1842

them under the same regulations as 'young persons' of thirteen to eighteen. The hours for children under thirteen were further reduced, to six and a half a day, and dangerous machinery had to be fenced. Ashley's great aim, a ten-hour day, was achieved for women and young persons in the mills in 1847, although it was changed to ten and a half in 1850. Because the work could not be carried on by men alone, this had the effect of reducing men's hours as well.

The factory owners said the limitation of hours would ruin the textile industry. Some claimed their profit was made in the last hour of the day, so that they could not afford to work a shorter time. Yet, within a few years, they had to admit that the Factory Acts actually increased output. The workers were more efficient now that they were not so exhausted by long hours. The rest of the nineteenth century saw continued progress in factory reform. Earlier Acts were extended beyond textiles to apply to other industries, including workshops. Disraeli's Government further reduced hours in 1874—to a maximum of fifty-six a week (ten hours Monday to Friday and six on Saturday). Meanwhile, more factory inspectors were appointed, with wider powers, and safety regulations were tightened.

By this time, workers were more capable of protecting themselves through their trade unions. The Government did not interfere in wages disputes between employers and workmen, but it gave the unions the legal protection necessary for them to fight most of their own battles. Thus the State, encouraged by a few individuals, had gradually accepted greater responsibility for the well-being of the people in their places of work. Later factory reforms were accepted not as interference with people's liberty, but as essential to an increase of freedom by releasing workers from the bondage of their machines.

Public health and housing

The Factory Acts improved conditions where people worked. At least of equal importance was the question of living conditions in the industrial towns. The population of Britain doubled between 1780 and 1830, and was to double again by 1890. This caused enormous problems of overcrowding in unhealthy houses. The connection between dirt and disease had long been known, but improvements were held up by lack of scientific knowledge and insufficient government powers. No one was safe from the lack of proper sanitation. Prince Albert, the Queen's husband, died in 1861 from typhoid, a direct result of drinking impure water.

Edwin Chadwick (1800–90) the First Secretary of the Poor

Edwin Chadwick—sanitary reformer

Law Commission, revealed that a great deal of poverty was caused by disease and ill health. Thus the workhouses could become as great a burden on the rates as the earlier forms of poor relief had been unless the spread of disease was checked by better sanitation. Chadwick wanted the Government to take responsibility for improving public health. He compiled a Report on the Sanitary Condition of the Labouring Population (1842) which said:

'Disease . . . is always found in connection with damp and filth, and close and overcrowded dwellings . . . and where these circumstances are removed by drainage, proper cleansing, better ventilation . . . the frequency of such disease is abated (lessened) . . .

'The annual loss of life from filth and bad ventilation is greater than the loss from death or wounds in any wars in which the country has been engaged in modern times.'

Chadwick's argument, that it was better to prevent poverty caused by ill health than to spend money on poor relief when the damage was done, was certain to appeal to ratepayers. Nevertheless, it took a severe outbreak of cholera in 1847 to spur the Government into action. The first Public Health Act (1848) set up a Board of Health in London which could order the establishment of local boards around the country. These would have powers over necessary services like cleansing, draining and paving the streets. Nothing was compulsory, however, and when the Board of Health was disbanded, six years later, only a sixth of the population was served by local boards. Even so, opportunities had been created for local action and, where this was taken, epidemic disease was greatly reduced.

Meanwhile, Chadwick took a hand himself, experimenting with glazed earthenware pipes for making sewers. He found them vastly better than the brick-lined tunnels then in use. Pipes prevented blockages, and they were soon regarded as essential for all sanitary engineering. Chadwick stressed the need for greater government powers if really large-scale improvements were to be achieved. However, many ratepayers were opposed to any form of centralised control. Not until 1871, with the formation of the Local Government Board, was there an effective central authority to co-ordinate all sanitary, public health and poor law services throughout the country.

The climax of mid-Victorian concern with sanitation was the 1875 Public Health Act, passed by Disraeli's Ministry. It set up a uniform service of sanitary authorities throughout the whole country. They were responsible for sewerage, water supply and refuse disposal, among other things. In every locality, Medical Officers of Health and Sanitary Inspectors were to be appointed, under the central control of the Local Government Board. By the turn of the century, British towns were much healthier, although still far below present-day standards. The average expectation of life increased by ten years between 1850 and 1900—a measure of the rapid progress in public health. By this time, most of the basic sanitary services were established and the public health problem had become largely a housing problem.

The demand for houses was greater than the supply right through the nineteenth century; as, indeed, it still is today. The enormous increase in population caused terrible overcrowding. The 1891 census found that over ten per cent of the people lived more than two to a room. Yet not until 1868

Blue Gate Fields—a London slum in the 1870s

was any attempt made to give town councils power to deal with housing. Even then very little was achieved, for the authorities were reluctant to interfere with private property. Sanitary improvements did not meet this obstacle. This was no problem in the case of most sanitary improvements because they did not threaten a landlord's property—on the contrary they increased its value.

As a young man, Benjamin Disraeli had urged the State to use its powers to protect industrial workers. Some thirty years later, he tried to turn words into actions. In 1875 his Government passed an Artisans' Dwellings Act which gave councils powers to take over and clear whole slum areas. Although it was not compulsory, some councils acted promptly. In London, nearly 30,000 were rehoused in the next thirty years, and in Birmingham, under its great mayor, Joseph Chamberlain, over forty acres of slum land were purchased for £1,500,000 and cleared.

Unfortunately many of the cleared sites became, in the words of one observer, 'a cemetery for cats and a last resting place for worn-out boots and kettles' before private builders could be found to redevelop the land. Local authorities were not urged to build houses themselves until 1890. Even then, little was done until after the 1914–18 war. It was all very well to outlaw slums, but replacing them with better houses, at rents within the reach of everyone, was not so easy.

Central and local government

Up to 1867, only about one man in ten could vote in parliamentary elections (no women at all until 1919). The right to vote was based on property and wealth, so that the upper and middle classes had almost a monopoly of political power. However, when the State was doing so much more to improve conditions for the workers, it seemed common sense to give them a share in deciding who should rule. In 1867, therefore, a Parliamentary Reform Act almost doubled the electorate and redistributed the seats in favour of the expanding towns. All male householders in the boroughs could now vote. A further Act of 1884 put agricultural labourers on the same footing as town workers by giving the vote to householders in the counties. These two Acts together extended the vote to most adult males.

17

In addition, the corrupt system of open voting was replaced by secret ballot in 1872. There was now no need for a man to declare his political views in public and risk offending those in authority over him. It was not a coincidence that reform of the House of Commons in the last third of the nineteenth century was accompanied by a quickening in the pace of social reform. Ordinary working men formed the majority of the electorate after 1884, and could therefore bring great pressure to bear on the policies of the political parties.

In step with these developments, the system of local government was also reshaped. No social reform could be effective without well-organised local authorities to carry out the day-to-day administration. Borough Councils, elected by the ratepayers, had been active in the industrial towns since the 1830s. Birmingham, under Joseph Chamberlain, showed how

Joseph Chamberlain—mayor of Birmingham and social reformer

effective the best of them could be. As Chamberlain said, Birmingham 'was parked, paved, assized, marketed, gas and watered and improved—all as a result of three years active work'.

Progress was slower in the countryside. Even in the 1880s country dwellers had little say in the running of their locality. An important Local Government Act (1888) remedied this by setting up elected County Councils. Some sixty large towns were released from the influence of the County Councils and made separate County Boroughs, with their own local self-government. London became a separate county. A further Act of 1894 established nearly 7,000 Parish Councils and also the system of Urban and Rural District Councils, all based on direct election by the people. The strengthening of local government was a necessary first step before any kind of Welfare State, as we know it, could be established.

As the Victorian Age drew to a close, the people could look back on well over half a century of reform. Parliament had helped to secure improvements in the mines, factories and workshops. Trade unions were given legal protection, and the vote had been extended to every male householder. Public sanitary services were well established and a start had been made on the problem of slum clearance. Though the worker's lot was still harsh by modern standards, it was much better than it had ever been. It was from these reforms that the State's concern with the problems of living in an industrial society had its first cautious origins.

3 'Board School Brats'

No matter how much working conditions and living standards were improved, the labouring classes could never develop into full and equal members of society without education. Nevertheless, throughout most of the nineteenth century, the Government made little effort to provide schools. Education was still a private affair which had to be paid for, often at a high price. Although this did not present any problem for wealthy parents, most working people could not afford to pay school fees. In any case, they needed to get their children out to work at an early age to help make up the family income.

Voluntary schools

Early in the nineteenth century, various private and charity schools were established to cater for working-class children. Well-meaning ladies sometimes held small classes in their homes for about twopence a week. The instruction in these 'dame schools' was usually dull and mechanical, and often worthless. In the absence of government regulations, there was nothing to stop anyone from opening a school, however ignorant he was. Thomas Wood, son of a Yorkshire weaver, wrote this about his education by an old man in the 1820s: 'I only remember one book . . . a big Bible. The little ones learnt letters out of it. Bigger ones learnt to read. I am not quite sure we ever read anything but the first chapter of St John . . . My school life came to an end when I was about eight years old.'

Many people thought the poor needed instruction in religion, which meant reading the Bible. Church societies therefore began to run free elementary schools, but only in some areas. There was great rivalry between the Nonconformist 'British and Foreign Schools Society' (1808) and the Church of England 'National Society for the Education of the Poor' (1811). Both were short of money and teachers, so they operated a 'monitorial system'. One master taught a select

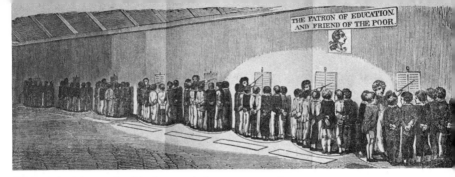

'The monitorial system'—older boys teach the younger ones in groups

group of older pupils, the monitors, and these, in turn, taught the juniors. One of the founders of this system, Andrew Bell, said: 'Give me twenty-four pupils today, and I will give you twenty-four teachers tomorrow.' It was possible for one master to supervise the teaching of hundreds of pupils by this method—but there was no guarantee that they learned anything.

In addition, there were some factory schools, Sunday schools (for children who worked all the week) and, later, workhouse schools. None of these aimed to teach more than 'habits of industry and piety' to children of the poor. Pupils were to know their duty and keep their place. However, in spite of these developments, a large majority of children received no education at all when Queen Victoria came to the throne (1837). The first sign of government interest was a grant of £20,000 to the Church Societies in 1833 for school building. The grant was increased to £30,000 in 1839 and a special Education Committee set up. Even then, the Government was spending more in a year on the Queen's stables than on the education of the poor!

The Secretary of the Education Committee, James Kay Shuttleworth, thought lack of education was an important cause of poverty and ill health. He said the poor were too ignorant to look after themselves properly, and the Government should take more responsibility for providing them with schools. Kay Shuttleworth was not satisfied with the 'monitorial system', so he made great efforts to increase the supply of trained teachers. He started a Teachers' Training College at Battersea, and, from this good example, voluntary colleges sprang up in other areas. To get over the immediate teacher shortage, Kay Shuttleworth began a 'pupil teacher' system, which he had seen working successfully in Holland. Pupil teachers were like apprentices. During the day they helped the older teachers, and in their spare time they studied themselves and took lessons, usually from the headmaster. After five years they took exams to become assistant teachers or qualify for a training college.

Education was still little more than elementary religious knowledge and the bare essentials of reading and writing. Anything more was regarded as extravagance, although Kay Shuttleworth thought the working man needed more, to enrich his drab life. He appointed more inspectors (there were only two in 1839) and expanded teachers' training facilities. By the middle of the century, State grants had risen to £500,000 a year. The middle classes were now more prepared to accept the idea of government aid for elementary education. There was a growing need in industry for people who could read and write. Also, it was widely believed that crime, unrest and drunkenness in the towns were direct results of ignorance, and that uneducated workers might be a danger to the peace and security of the nation.

While there was no proper State system of education, however, the voluntary schools went on expanding, through the efforts of generous and far-sighted individuals. One of these we have already met as a factory reformer—Lord Ashley. By about 1850, with the ten-and-a-half-hour day achieved, Ashley began to take an interest in the Ragged Schools Union. This was an organisation to provide a little free education for the children of poor parents. Ashley soon became President, and set about building new schools and improving old ones. He raised funds to provide food and clothing as well for those in dire need, and even resorted to begging money from M.P.s as they entered Parliament, to help finance his schemes. He put so much of his own money into charitable work that he was often penniless, but this did not trouble him. He once said: 'I would rather be President of the Ragged Schools Union than have the command of armies or wield the destiny of empires.'

For all their efforts, however, the voluntary schools could not alone cope with the demand for education. The State would have to do more. Reformers had long suggested that schools should be built out of the local rates, but the Government was slow to act because of the difficulties involved. The wealthy were reluctant to tax themselves in order to pay for the education of their social inferiors, and the Churches had been squabbling among themselves for thirty years on the subject of how the available money should be spent. Rate-payers who belonged to the Church of England objected to paying rates to support schools which did not teach their religion, while Nonconformists took a similar view when they were asked to give aid to Church of England schools.

'Payment by results'

In 1861 a Royal Commission on Education suggested a system of paying grants to schools, 'out of the county rates, in consideration of the attainment of a certain degree of knowledge by the children in the school during the year preceding the payment'. Robert Lowe, Vice-President of the Department of Education, liked this idea. It promised something definite in return for money spent. As he put it: 'If it is not cheap, it shall be efficient; if it is not efficient, it shall be cheap.' In the following year, therefore, his Revised Code established a system of 'payment by results'.

Inspectors visited grant-aided schools each year to examine children in the 'three Rs' (reading, 'riting and 'rithmetic) and up to twelve shillings per child was paid on the result of the examination. Teachers, realising the importance of the occasion, often resorted to underhand methods—like signalling the answers to the children from behind the inspector's back. 'Payment by results' certainly helped to even out standards from one district to another, and in some cases made the teachers more efficient, but it was a bad system in many respects. For example, bright children were neglected while the teacher concentrated on bringing the slower ones up to the required standard.

By this time, just under half of the nation's $3\frac{1}{2}$ million children were getting some kind of schooling. Apart from the religious disagreements, further progress was hampered by doubts about whether schools should be paid for out of the rates. Another Royal Commission (1868) put both sides of the argument. On the one hand, 'it is a matter of national interest that intellectual ability, in whatever rank it may be found, should have the fullest opportunities of cultivation'. But, against this view, 'it seems more likely that people will learn the value of education by being perpetually urged to make the sacrifices necessary to procure it for their children, than by being set free from all care or labour for the purpose'.

The thing which really tipped the scales was the 1867 Parliamentary Reform Act, which gave the vote to working-class householders in the boroughs. Robert Lowe said, 'We must educate our future masters.' By this he meant that the new voters should at least be able to read and write before they chose their Member of Parliament. Another factor was the great strides being made in education in other countries—especially Germany and the United States, which had become our main trading rivals. Britain's industrial supremacy was sure to be lost if half her children remained uneducated. It was time for decisive government action.

Board Schools

An Education Act of 1870 was the turning point. Parliament ordered the election of local School Boards in all districts where proper schools were not already provided by the religious societies. These Boards could provide elementary schools for the five to ten age group, paid for out of the local rates. Parents were to be excused fees if they were very poor, although attendance was not compulsory. The Boards were to assist in the maintenance of the Church schools, but not in the building of them, which went on as before, with the aid of direct government grants. Thus Parliament had at last taken responsibility for the education of the nation's children. Most of the schools were drab and badly equipped, and classes of eighty or ninety were common, but at least it was the start of some sort of 'system'.

Sherlock Holmes, in one of Conan Doyle's famous detective stories, said of the Board Schools: 'Lighthouses, my boy! Beacons of the future! Capsules, with hundreds of bright little seeds in each, out of which will spring the wiser, better England of the future.' He was correct in his prediction, although, at the time, most of the pupils were far from being 'bright little seeds'. They were mostly dirty and ragged, with skin diseases and running noses and ears. More fortunate

Boys of the same age in a school in Bermondsey, London, in 1894 (above) and 1924 (below)

middle-class children, from expensive private schools, called them 'Board School Brats'. Before the 'brats' could be educated, they had to be civilised. Schooling encouraged habits of punctuality, discipline and cleanliness which, in time, increased their self-respect and made them less hostile to 'book learning'.

By 1880 there were enough schools to make possible compulsory attendance up to the age of ten (gradually raised to twelve by the end of the century). Many parents objected to this, saying they could not afford to lose the wages of their

An arithmetic class, 1891

children, if they had started work. To make compulsory attendance possible, many Boards had to arrange for cheap school meals and medical attention, along with the distribution of charity clothing for the most ragged ones. Fees were low, but many families still had great difficulty finding the money. Even a penny or twopence a week was a lot of money

26

when the difference between weekly earnings and the rent was often only two or three shillings. Therefore, elementary education was made free in 1891.

Beginnings of State secondary education

So far we have only considered elementary, or primary, education. Until the end of the nineteenth century there was no question of providing secondary education for the poor. This was restricted to those who could afford the fees of private, grammar or public schools. But clever children from Board schools needed something more than just elementary education. By the 1890s, some Boards provided 'higher grade schools', and County Councils were allowed to support technical, evening and other advanced classes. However, these opportunities were open to only a small proportion of the working class.

At last, by the Education Act of 1902, Parliament made secondary schools the concern of the State. The Boards were abolished and their duties taken over by County and County Borough Councils. They had done well, providing nearly $2\frac{1}{2}$ million school places, but most Boards were too small to be really efficient. The new Local Education Authorities could now create their own secondary schools, charging small fees. However, from 1907, some free scholarship places were left open to the cleverest children from the elementary schools. Government grants helped to take some of the extra financial burden off the local rates.

Thus free secondary education was now available for those who could show themselves worthy of it. But there were very few 'free places' at first. Even by 1914, less than one in twenty from the elementary schools won a 'scholarship' to secondary school. Nevertheless, education for the poor had come a long way since the days of the 'monitorial system'. There was a general feeling of reform in the early years of the new century. Working people demanded more and more a higher standard of living. As they became better educated they found ways of voicing their opinions—not just through trade unions, but through political organisations like the Labour Party (founded in 1906). The forces of education, once let loose, could not be contained.

27

4 Poverty in York, 1899

Before we leave the Victorian Age behind, two important questions need to be asked. First, what effect had the nineteenth-century reforms had on the standards of working-class life? Second, what further improvements were still urgently required? We can arrive at some of the answers by trying to find out how much poverty still existed in Britain at the turn of the century, and the reasons for it.

B. Seebohm Rowntree

To make the picture more sharply defined we will focus on just one city, York, through the eyes of Seebohm Rowntree, who made a special study of its working classes in 1899. Seebohm, as you may have guessed, was the son of a cocoa and chocolate manufacturer. He began work as a chemist in the family business in 1889, at the age of eighteen. In the same year, a book was published which was to make a great impression on him. It was the first of a seventeen-volume survey by Charles Booth, a Liverpool shipowner, on *The Life and Labour of the People of London*. Booth discovered that about a third of London's population lived in deep poverty, earning about £1 a week or less.

Like his father, Seebohm soon became greatly concerned with the problems of working-class life, especially the extent and causes of poverty. He decided before long to conduct a survey of his own to compare conditions in a smaller town with those found in London by Booth. As he put it: 'One knows there is a great deal of poverty in the East End of London but I wonder whether there is in provincial cities. Why not investigate York?' Certainly, if Rowntree could show that a thick layer of poverty existed in an ancient city like York, it would make the public and the Government take notice and prove wrong many of Booth's critics who claimed London was exceptional.

Thus, early in 1899, with the aid of an interviewer and a

secretary, Rowntree began a house-to-house inquiry, extending to the whole working-class population of York. This involved 46,754 people, two-thirds of the total population. The keeping of servants was taken as the dividing line between the working classes and those of a higher social rank.

The extent of poverty

Rowntree found 20,302 people living in a state of poverty. In other words, almost twenty-eight per cent, or two people in every seven, did not have enough food, fuel and clothing to keep them in good health. Since this was almost half of York's entire working-class population, there could be no question but that the Victorian reformers had left a great deal of problems unsolved. Of those in poverty, about a third did not have enough money coming in each week to live a normal, healthy life *even if they spent every penny wisely.* All the traditional Victorian 'remedies' like thrift were no use to these people. You could not be expected to save money when you did not have enough for basic essentials. The remaining two-thirds had enough income to give them the bare necessities, but they spent some portion of it unwisely. As a result, they were forced to go short on food or clothing, or both.

These figures were very close to those arrived at by Charles Booth. He had found just over thirty per cent in poverty in East London, working on roughly the same definition of poverty as Rowntree. Therefore it certainly seemed likely that almost a third of Britain's town dwellers were forced to go without some of the necessities of a civilised life. The terrible effect of this on the health and well-being of the people can be seen from the fact that a third of the men applying to join the army at this time were rejected as unfit. These conditions were not confined to the towns. A few years later, Rowntree found that agricultural labourers were even worse off.

What was it like living in poverty? Rowntree found that most of the families in this situation could afford nothing better than a damp, dark slum. Often one water tap supplied several houses and, in many cases, this was fixed to the wall of the W.C.! 'Midden privvies' were the general rule in the slums. In these the functions of lavatory and dustbin were

Elegance and squalor—York Minster surrounded by crowded slums

combined in a brick-lined pit. Rowntree said: 'A large number of them are found inches deep in liquid filth, or so full of refuse as to reach above the cemented portions of the walls.' To make matters worse, they were often shared by several families.

Broken window panes were stuffed with rags or pasted over with brown paper. In the neighbourhood of these houses, the smell from dirt and bad air could be almost unbearable. This is a typical example of living conditions taken from a Sanitary Inspector's notebook: '2 rooms. In the lower one a brick floor is in holes. Fireplace without grate in bottom. Wooden floor of upper room has large holes admitting numbers of mice. Roof very defective, rain falling through on to the bed in wet weather.'

In these conditions, it was not surprising that one child out of every four born died before it was a year old and many of those that lived were stunted and deformed. As Rowntree put it: 'It is Nature's universal law that all living things tend

30

to adapt themselves to their environment' (surroundings). Public Health and Housing Acts still left much to be desired. There was not even a full-time Medical Officer of Health in York until 1900.

The diet of the poverty-stricken slum dwellers was often seriously deficient. Many families could afford no butcher's meat at all. Rowntree asked some of the housewives to keep accounts of the money they spent and the menus provided. Here is a typical example of a family in poverty:

	BREAKFAST	LUNCH/DINNER	TEA	SUPPER
SATURDAY	Bread, butter, boiled egg, coffee	Meat, potatoes, pie, tea	Bread, butter, tea	Roast potatoes, tea
SUNDAY	Bread, butter, coffee	Beef, potatoes, pudding, tea	Bread, butter, tea	Meat, bread, tea
MONDAY	Bread, butter, coffee	Meat, potatoes, bread, tea	Bread, butter, tea	
TUESDAY	Bread, butter, tea	Hash, bread, tea	Bread, butter, tea	
WEDNESDAY	Bread, butter, coffee	Liver, potatoes, onions, tea	Bread, butter, tea, dripping	
THURSDAY	Bread, butter, coffee	Bread, dripping, tea	Bread, dripping, tea	
FRIDAY	Bread, butter, tea	Bread, butter, toast, tea	Toast, butter, tea	

This meagre diet accounted for almost half the family's total income; the rest going mainly on fuel and rent. Although it may have contained enough bulk to fight off the feeling of hunger, it did not contain sufficient nourishment to keep the family in good health. Notice how it tails off towards the end of the week. From looking at the family menu you can work out the day on which the father was paid. Extras like clothing often had to be paid for by going short of food. One woman said: 'If there's anything extra to buy, such as a pair of boots for one of the children, me and the children goes without dinner.'

Many families above the 'poverty line' at the time of the survey had earlier been in poverty when their children were too young to work. When children's wages were so important for the family's living standards it is easy to see why there were so many objections to compulsory education. Children were taken away from school at the earliest possible moment. One boy in a Board School asked his teacher:

' "Please, sir, what time is it?"

' "Half-past ten, my lad, but what's the matter?"

' "Please, sir, then may I go, sir? My mother said I should be fourteen at ten-thirty this morning, and I could leave school when I was fourteen, sir." '

In fact, no School Board had been established in York until 1889; nineteen years after the 1870 Act ordered Boards to be set up! Ten years later, however, there were twenty-one free elementary schools in York.

Hundreds of people, especially old folk, were only kept out of the workhouse by private charity or assistance from relatives. Some families went short themselves in order to offer poor relations a home. Even so, York's workhouse had about 450 inhabitants; and a further 1,000 received poor relief in their homes. The 'able-bodied' in the workhouse mainly chopped and bundled wood for sale in the city. Children went to elementary school when they were old enough, but, for the rest of the time, they mixed with the adults—often learning bad habits from them.

The causes of poverty

Taking those whose basic incomes were insufficient, Rowntree found two main reasons for their plight. In a quarter of these cases, the chief wage-earner of the family was out of action or dead. He might be ill or disabled, too old to work or unemployed. However, in over half the families in this category, the breadwinner was in regular work. His wages were simply too low to meet his family's needs. Unskilled labourers earned roughly eighteen to twenty-one shillings a week in York at this time, yet Rowntree estimated that at least 21s 8d was needed to keep a family with three children out of poverty. The belief that a man could always provide for his family if he was thrifty and willing to work hard was shown to be false. However hard he tried, he could not keep out of poverty if he was seriously underpaid.

In the case of those whose incomes were sufficient but who failed to spend every penny wisely, it was more difficult to give definite reasons for their poverty. Drink and gambling—in that order—were almost certainly the main causes. When father drank, the children often went supperless to bed. Rowntree deplored these vices, but suggested that men often took to drink and gambling not from weakness of character but because of the terrible conditions under which they lived. Extravagant housekeeping was another cause of unnecessary poverty. Housewives often spent unwisely through ignorance of what was the best value for money.

Judging from conditions in York, it appeared that the Victorian reforms, although a valuable start, had not removed the root causes of poverty. The most urgent problem was low wages, but no Government wanted to interfere with the right of an employer to pay his workers what he thought fit. Workmen would have to fight their own battles through their trade unions. Nevertheless, many reformers, Rowntree included, thought employers should be forced to pay some kind of national minimum wage.

Rowntree's findings led many people to look beyond mere *public* health to *personal* health and welfare services. The lives of the poor were precarious. They needed insurances and pensions to give them a regular income when they were not earning. Better-off workers could afford to contribute to insurance schemes run by trade unions and Friendly Societies, but few unskilled workers could spare the money for subscriptions to such schemes. The State would have to help these people. The challenge for the twentieth century was clear. It would take all the wisdom and understanding of the people to meet it.

PART TWO: UNFINISHED BUSINESS, 1906–39

5 Foundation Stones

The early years of the twentieth century, up to the Great War of 1914–18, marked a turning point in the social history of Britain. Parliament at last turned its attention from empire-building overseas to the problem of poverty on its own doorstep. This policy had been recommended back in 1890 by 'General' William Booth, founder of the Salvation Army. In his book *Darkest England*, he suggested that the 'white man's burden' of civilising Africans and other backward peoples of the world should begin at home, in the industrial towns, where wretched slum dwellers were forced to live like savages.

In 1902, an American writer, Jack London, lived for a time among the poor of the East End of London. He found that most wages were too low for people to live decently. Thousands walked the streets, day and night, without proper food and shelter, because of a general shortage of both work and housing. He warned the British that their country would suffer a serious decline if workmen continued to live in these conditions: 'Brutalised, degraded and dull, . . . It is absurd to think for an instant that they can compete with the workers of the New World.' The rot had already set in. Nearly half the volunteers for the army during the Boer War (1899–1902) were rejected because of ill health. In London, one adult worker in every three died on public charity—in a workhouse, hospital or asylum.

' The Liberal landslide'

The wealthy, secure in their world of plenty, were still not disturbed. They said poverty would die out of its own accord as Britain got richer. This mean, heartless attitude was, however, strongly attacked by the Liberal Party in Parliament. Out of office since 1895, they were determined to make war on poverty once they got back to power. It was not good enough just to wait for things to get better of their own accord. In the general election of 1905, working-class voters put their faith in the Liberals, helping them to gain a massive majority. The way was now clear for them to carry out their policy of reform.

There were many able men in the new ministry, not least among them David Lloyd George and Winston Churchill.

David Lloyd George—'father of the welfare state'

Lloyd George, often called 'the father of the Welfare State', had a greater knowledge of the real needs of working people than any Cabinet Minister before him. 'In so far as poverty is

35

due to circumstances over which man has no control,' he said, 'then the State should step in to the very utmost limit of its resources.' When Lloyd George became Chancellor of the Exchequer in 1908, Winston Churchill took over from him as President of the Board of Trade, at the early age of thirty-three. There was no doubt where his sympathies lay. 'The cause of Liberalism is the cause of the left-out millions,' he said.

Child welfare

In the next few years, the Liberals laid the foundations for the Welfare State. The needs of children were their first priority, for the best way of improving the physical condition of the people was to start with the rising generation. The birth rate had declined rapidly since the 1870s, so that people were now less prepared to accept the yearly loss of well over 100,000 lives in infancy. Clean water and better sanitation were not enough; babies needed clean food and milk if they were to escape disease, and mothers required guidance. A number of local authorities had recently opened clean milk depots and appointed Health Visitors to advise parents on infant care. After 1906, with government assistance, infant welfare clinics were opened in many areas. The value of these improvements can be seen in the following figures:

INFANT DEATH RATE
(per 1,000 births)

1901	151
1905	128
1912	95

It is now below twenty per thousand, which shows how much room for improvement still remained after 1912.

Older children had been partly the responsibility of the whole community ever since Parliament compelled them to go to school. Compulsory education itself exposed still further the evils of poverty. Hordes of ragged, diseased and starving children now came into the public eye, instead of hiding away in the dingy slums where their plight was ignored. As a result, in many towns, charity organisations provided meals for children who were too hungry to learn, and clothing for the most ragged ones.

Free dinners for poor children, 1889

The Liberals now wished to extend school meals to all areas. By an Act of 1906, Local Education Authorities could either make use of existing voluntary schemes or, where these were absent, provide meals themselves. An extra halfpenny could be put on the rates for this purpose. Only children who were 'unable by reason of lack of food to take full advantage of the education provided for them' received meals, but it was still an important step forward. 'I'm not used to having a Sunday dinner every day' was a common remark from children in the early days of the scheme. By 1914, over 150,000 children had school meals—on Saturdays and during the holidays as well as in term-time.

Under-nourishment was only part of a general health problem among children. A Royal Commission (1909) reported that:

'Nearly the whole of the children of a slum quarter may go on year after year suffering from adenoids, inflamed glands, enlarged tonsils, defects of eyesight, chronic ear discharges . . . which will eventually prevent many of them from earning their livelihood.'

From 1907, local authorities were compelled to have children in elementary schools medically examined. As a result, many appalling facts came to light. In Liverpool, for example, over eighty per cent of the girls examined were infested with bugs, fleas and lice. Parents were made responsible for

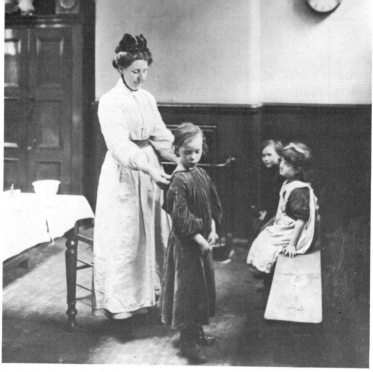

A child being medically inspected, 1912

obtaining the necessary treatment for their children, but many of them neglected their duty. Therefore, the Board of Education gave grants, after 1912, to make more treatment possible.

The Government's concern for the welfare of children extended beyond their schooldays. Juvenile Employment Bureaux were started in 1910 to help leavers find suitable jobs. These were only part of a whole new structure of services catering for the special needs of the young. Borstals and Probation Courts were introduced by the Liberals (1909) in the hope of preventing young offenders from hardening into criminals. Imprisonment of children was abolished. The emphasis was, rightly, on prevention rather than punishment. The new attitude to the young even extended to making it an offence to allow children to beg, or buy cigarettes.

Old age pensions and 'The People's Budget'

The idea of a State pensions scheme had been discussed in Britain ever since Germany introduced one in 1889. Bismarck, then German Chancellor, said it was unfair to give soldiers pensions whilst allowing 'the veterans of industry to die in misery'. However, Conservative Governments claimed the State could not stand the great cost. This is not surprising, considering the vast sums of money being spent overseas at the end of the nineteenth century. The cost of financing the Boer War alone would have paid for an adequate pensions scheme for about a quarter of a century.

When they came to power, the Liberals promised old age pensions as soon as they could spare the money. By 1908, a way was found to finance a State scheme which, in the words of the new Prime Minister, H. H. Asquith, had been 'long deserved and long deferred'. Pensions were granted to the over-seventies, provided they were British subjects and their income was not above twelve shillings a week. The pension varied between one and five shillings weekly, depending on the pensioner's income. Payments were made at post offices. Old people had no cause to feel shame at being given public money. Pensions, unlike poor relief, were paid as a right.

Pensions were the first truly nationwide social service. The Government admitted that the weekly payments were small but said they could not afford more. 'We have not pretended

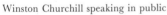

Winston Churchill speaking in public

to carry the toiler on to dry land,' said Churchill. 'What we have done is to strap a lifebelt around him.' Even so, he pointed out that: 'Nearly eight millions of money are being sent circulating through unusual channels, long frozen by poverty; circulating in the homes of the poor, flowing through the little shops that cater to their needs.' Old people were delighted to have this regular income. They were now less dependent on the goodwill of relations or the grudging help of the poor law. As Lloyd George said: 'We are lifting the shadow of the workhouse from the homes of the poor.'

To pay for social welfare schemes, especially pensions, Lloyd George estimated that an extra £16,000,000 would have to be raised in taxes. Introducing his budget of 1909, he said: 'This is a war budget. It is for raising money to wage implacable warfare on poverty and squalidness.' As well as increased taxes on drink and tobacco, and a new motor-car licence, Lloyd George raised the income tax. It was scaled, so that the rich paid 1s 2d in the pound while those with incomes below £3,000 a year paid only ninepence. A further 'super-

Punch cartoon showing Lloyd George as he must have appeared to the wealthy ruling class (plutocrats) after his budget

RICH FARE.

The Giant Lloyd-Gorgibuster: "FEE, FI, FO, FAT,
I SMELL THE BLOOD OF A PLUTOCRAT;
BE HE ALIVE OR BE HE DEAD,
I'LL GRIND HIS BONES TO MAKE MY BREAD."

tax' of sixpence in the pound was levied on the rich. In addition, Lloyd George placed a series of heavy taxes on profits gained from property—for example, rents and sales of land.

The 'People's Budget', as it was called, raised a storm of opposition from the wealthy classes. Income tax increases were bad enough, but property taxes were more than they would stand for. The Conservatives, many of them landowners, used their majority in the House of Lords to reject the budget. This disgusted the Liberals. They pointed out that the people who lived most extravagantly always seemed to object strongest to any increase in government spending. After a long struggle, the Government forced the Lords to accept the budget. Soon afterwards, the Parliament Act (1911) drastically reduced the powers of the House of Lords for the future. The cause of social reform had won the day! Increased government spending on the welfare of the needy had become an established principle.

Unemployment and labour exchanges

There had been signs of a new approach to the problem of unemployment in the previous Conservative ministry. In 1897 Parliament made it compulsory for some employers to pay compensation to injured workmen. The Liberals extended Workmen's Compensation (1906) to include all injuries at work and even some industrial diseases. Another Conservative measure, the Unemployed Workmen Act (1905) attempted for the first time to deal with unemployment on a nationwide scale. Local authorities could form Distress Committees in each borough. Work was provided, where possible, and in suitable cases emigration was arranged. The Liberals renewed the Act, granting £200,000 from the Treasury to increase local funds. From now on, unemployment was a national responsibility.

William Beveridge, a young civil servant, made a close study of unemployment and put forward some valuable suggestions. He had been greatly impressed by German 'labour exchanges', where both employers and workmen registered their requirements. By this means, the unemployed could be made aware of any vacancies which existed. The idea was not

A new labour exchange, 1910

entirely new in Britain, but Beveridge's plan was more ambitious than anything attempted before. He soon converted Churchill to the idea, and, early in 1910, the first eighty-three labour exchanges opened. They were part of a wider scheme, based on insurance, which was soon to be operated through them.

Unemployment insurance

The high spot of social reform in this period was the National Insurance Act of 1911. It was in two parts, the second dealing with unemployment. 'Through insurance', said Churchill, 'families can be secured against catastrophes which otherwise would smash them up for ever.' As we have seen, many workmen did insure themselves, through private organisations like Friendly Societies. However, poorly paid workers could not afford to pay sufficient subscriptions to give them adequate benefits. In any case, whether they could afford it or not, many preferred to 'take a chance' rather than pay for something they might never need. An irresponsible father could thus involve his family in great hardship if he lost his job. The Liberals hoped to bring insurance within the reach of those who needed it most by offering a State scheme, with higher benefits for lower contributions.

Because State insurance was a new departure—'a risky adventure into the unknown', Beveridge later called it—the 1911 scheme began on a small scale. Unemployment insurance was restricted to a few 'precarious' trades—building, ship-building, mechanical engineering, ironfounding, vehicle construction and sawmilling. If successful, the scheme was to be extended to other trades in the future. Workmen over sixteen, their employers and the State each contributed $2\frac{1}{2}d$ a week, thus spreading the cost over the whole community. In return, seven shillings a week was payable at a labour exchange from the second week of unemployment. This benefit continued for a maximum of fifteen weeks in any one year, provided enough contributions had been paid beforehand.

William Beveridge here describes some further details of the scheme:

'We adopted the German plan of raising contributions from employers and employees by stamps attached to cards; but we should almost certainly have been forced to think of that ourselves. . . . In so far as we used any working models we used the trade unions—in particular their practice of requiring signature of a vacant book in working hours as proof of unemployment, and their common provision of a waiting period before benefit began.'

Benefits were not enough to provide a living on their own and, in any case, there was a time limit on them. Thus workers were not encouraged to remain idle—they still needed to find a job as soon as possible. Taken all round, the scheme was a great success. Unlike poor relief, workmen paid part of the cost of unemployment insurance themselves. Thus they did not have the feeling of 'living on charity' when they were out of work.

Health insurance

Part I of the 1911 Act was another long-awaited scheme 'to provide for insurance against loss of health and for prevention and cure of sickness.' Again, Germany provided the model.

43

Lloyd George had witnessed a great improvement in the condition of the German people as a result of health insurance, at very small cost to the State. 'I hope our competition with Germany will not be in armaments alone,' he said. As in the case of unemployment insurance, Friendly Society and trade union schemes had long been available to those who took the trouble and could afford the subscriptions. However, only about half of the working population was insured against sickness, and, even then, 250,000 policies lapsed every year because members failed to keep up regular payments. The uninsured had to get medical treatment under the poor law. It varied between fairly good care in some of the newest infirmaries to grudging reception into an old-fashioned mixed workhouse.

'The community must lend its powerful aid,' said Lloyd George. However, there were problems to be overcome first— especially the opposition of doctors to the plan. They were mostly in favour of a State medical service, but thought they should run it themselves. The Government, on the other hand, wished to operate through the Friendly Societies; creating so-called 'approved societies'. After much argument, which threatened to wreck the whole plan, a compromise was reached which gave doctors better conditions than they had ever had before.

All wage-earners between sixteen and seventy had to belong to the scheme if they earned less than £3 a week. They paid fourpence a week, their employers threepence and the State added twopence. Stamps were stuck on individual cards. In return for these payments, free medical attention, with medicine, was given. This did not include hospital or specialist services, however, just 'simple doctoring'. When work was lost through sickness, ten shillings a week was paid by the approved society, from the fourth day of the illness. This lasted for twenty-six weeks, after which 'disablement benefit' of five shillings could be claimed. An additional thirty shillings 'maternity benefit' was paid on the birth of each child.

Most workmen were delighted at being given ninepence worth of insurance for fourpence, but there was some opposition. Many domestic servants claimed they were looked after and paid while they were sick without having to bother about

THE RIGHT TICKET FOR YOU!
YOU ARE TRAVELLING
ON A SAFE LINE

GOVERNMENT LINE
1913 MALE WORKER PAYS 4ᴰ
EMPLOYER PAYS 3ᴰ
STATE PAYS 2ᴰ

YOUR RETURN
DURING ILLNESS
10/- Per Week FOR 26 WEEKS
5/- AFTERWARDS (TILL 70) WHILE INCAPABLE OF WORK
FREE DOCTOR & MEDICINE
30/- Maternity Grant
SANATORIUM BENEFIT

AND ARE ASSURED
A SAFE RETURN

Leaflet explaining the new scheme of National Insurance against sickness, issued by the Government, 1911

insurance. Lloyd George replied that not everyone had such generous employers and it was therefore desirable for the whole community to co-operate in order to benefit those in the greatest need. 'Ladies' who employed servants said it was beneath their dignity to 'lick their stamps'. Not surprisingly, this hardship received little sympathy!

Churchill summed up the importance of both parts of the 1911 Act: 'The National Insurance Bill is the most decisive step yet taken upon the path of social organisation. . . . The cruel waste of disease and unemployment, breaking down men and women, breaking up homes and families, will for the first time be encountered by the whole strength of the nation.'

Minimum wages

The demands of Rowntree and others for a national minimum wage presented a great problem for the Government. Since low wages were probably the greatest single cause of poverty, it was likely that a legal minimum wage would do more than anything else to relieve misery. Nevertheless, the Liberals were certain to be called dictators if they tried to interfere with the sacred traditions of industry. They felt they must, as

45

THE DAWN OF HOPE.

Mr. LLOYD GEORGE'S National Health Insurance Bill provides for the insurance
of the Worker in case of Sickness.

Support the Liberal Government
in their policy of
SOCIAL REFORM.

Poster advertising National Health Insurance. The 'doctor' is
Lloyd George

a general rule, leave wages to be settled between employers
and trade unions.

However, they made two exceptions to the rule. The first
concerned miners, whose dangerous work for low wages gained
them great public sympathy. Parliament, having reduced
their working day to eight hours (1908), created a minimum
wage board for miners in 1912. The second exception involved
the so-called 'sweated' trades—for example, tailoring and
lace, chain and paper-box making. These workers, crammed
into tiny 'sweat shops', which were often little more than
attics, were the lowest paid of all. They were not organised
into trade unions, so they had no effective method of bargain-
ing for higher wages. To meet this need, Trade Boards were
set up by the Government, from 1909, to fix minimum wages
in the 'sweated' industries.

Churchill once defined the Liberal policy as 'drawing a line,
below which we will not allow persons to live and labour'.
Although the Government was reluctant to impose a general

minimum wage, its other policies went a long way towards achieving a minimum standard of living. By 1914 working people had five shillings between themselves and utter destitution in old age, and some of the dread of unemployment and sickness was removed by the knowledge that money would still be coming in. These reforms struck for the first time at the root causes of poverty. Instead of merely providing workhouses for the very worst cases, the Liberals had begun to develop more specialised services to meet individual needs. They had shown that the advantages of civilisation could be spread more evenly through government action than through individual effort.

6 The Shadow of Unemployment

The Great War of 1914–18 brought the period of Liberal reform to an end. Nevertheless, after Britain's 'bloodstained stagger to victory', as Lloyd George called it, the returning soldiers and their families looked forward to the future with high hopes. Lloyd George, Prime Minister since 1916, promised 'a land fit for heroes', with the wealth of the State being diverted from the demands of war to an all-out attack on poverty. The first signs were encouraging. Even before the peace treaty was signed, the vote was extended to all men over twenty-one, and even given to women for the first time— although they had to be over thirty and either ratepayers or the wives of ratepayers. A General Election was held almost immediately, and the wartime Coalition Government was returned to power with an enormous majority to continue its efforts in peacetime.

Unemployment insurance extended

Plans were soon made to expand the existing social services, starting with National Insurance against unemployment. The original scheme of 1911 had only covered a few 'precarious' industries. Although the number of trades was slightly enlarged in 1916, millions of workers were still left out. To remedy this, the Government introduced a much wider scheme in 1920. It covered everybody earning less than £5 a week, except farm labourers and domestic and civil servants. The insured paid fourpence a week, to which their employer added fourpence and the State twopence. Weekly benefits of fifteen shillings for men and twelve shillings for women could be claimed for up to fifteen weeks in any year—provided the labour exchange could not find them work. In the following year, allowances for 'dependants' were added: five shillings for a wife and a shilling for each child.

48

The depression begins

By 1921 life was practically back to normal. Everywhere people talked of 'business as usual'. Then, suddenly, the numbers of unemployed began to increase alarmingly. By the summer of 1921, two million men were out of work—one in every seven of working age. There was no immediate panic, however, for everyone expected the situation to improve very soon, as it usually had done in the past. They were not to know that British foreign trade was entering upon a period of rapid decline. From 1921 to 1940, the numbers of unemployed never fell below a million.

THE MOUNTAINEER.

RATEPAYER (*to the Premier*). "I KNOW YOU'RE ALWAYS KEEN ON MOUNTAINS, SIR. HAVE YOU NOTICED THIS ONE?"

This disastrous period of unemployment was all the more surprising because, for a short time after the war, British industry had enjoyed a 'boom' (increase of business). Every-

49

where there had been great demand for goods which had been scarce during wartime. However, by 1921, when more normal trading conditions returned, it was clear that Britain had lost many of her former overseas markets. Britain's share of world trade had been decreasing slowly for half a century, but there had never before been such a dramatic decline in so short a period. Many foreign customers, forced to find other sources of supply during the war, found they could now manage with less British goods. As a result, until Britain could find new customers or recover lost markets, there was simply not enough work to go round.

The timing of the trade depression was particularly unfortunate because the new system of unemployment insurance had already been worked out. It was based on the expectation of no more than four per cent out of work at any one time. In fact, the unemployment rate never fell below ten per cent for almost twenty years! Thus by the time the new scheme came into operation it was already out of date. Hundreds of thousands of workmen exhausted their fifteen weeks of benefit without any sign of a job. A further re-shaping of National Insurance was urgently needed if these men were to be kept off the poor law. However, throughout the 1920s, governments simply made adjustments to the original plan hoping the crisis would soon be over. 'Extended benefits'—nicknamed the 'dole'—were introduced as a temporary measure until the worst was over. But the worst was still to come, and extended benefits had themselves to be extended!

Unemployment did not affect the whole country equally. For the majority of people, the 1920s and 1930s was a period of steady improvement in wages and living standards. This was especially true of the areas with new, expanding industries, like building, electrical equipment and motor engineering, mostly in south-eastern England and the Midlands. The minority, who suffered grim unemployment, lived in areas of declining industry, mainly in the north of England and south Wales. Here the main industries were those that had made Britain a great industrial power in the nineteenth century—coal, iron and steel, shipbuilding and textiles. Unfortunately these were the hardest hit when Britain's share of overseas trade fell.

Life 'on the dole'

In the 'depressed areas', the long queue of unemployed outside the labour exchange, waiting to 'sign on', became a regular part of life. In his novel *Love on the Dole* (1933) Walter Greenwood described a typical scene at a labour exchange:

Queue of unemployed outside a labour exchange

'A dozen or so rows of chairs . . . were quickly occupied the instant the men rushed in. Those coming later lounged against the wall.

'When one of those seated was called to the counter, his immediate neighbour took his seat. The remainder, with much shuffling of feet and grating of chairs, all moved up a place so that none of the chairs ever were vacant, the queue waiting for them often stretching into the yard. The proceedings had come to be known as "musical chairs".'

Another novelist, George Orwell, toured the depressed areas in 1936, and described them in *The Road to Wigan Pier*. He was particularly struck by the patience and good sense shown by the people:

'. . . they realise that losing your job does not mean that

you cease to be a human being. Life is still fairly normal. . . . Instead of raging against their destiny, they have made things tolerable by lowering their standards. . . . You can't get much meat for threepence, but you can get a lot of fish-and-chips. . . . Milk costs threepence a pint and even "mild" beer costs fourpence, but . . . you can wring forty cups of tea out of a quarter-pound packet.'

Unemployed man who had not forgotten his sense of humour

There was a time limit on 'extended benefits'. When they finished, the only thing left was the poor law. Because of the large numbers of unemployed in the depressed areas, the Guardians paid 'outdoor relief'—money which could be claimed without having to enter the workhouse. However, because poor relief was financed out of the local rates, the ratepayers in the areas of high unemployment were very hard hit. There were over 600 Poor Law Unions in Britain, yet the main burden of the long-term unemployed fell on fewer than forty of them. The fairest solution to this problem was to take the long-term unemployed off the poor law altogether and make them the responsibility of the nation as a whole through national taxation. This was done, in stages, up to 1934, by which time relief of the unemployed had been taken right out of local hands.

The depression gets worse—the 'means test'

A worldwide financial crisis, beginning with the collapse of the American stock market in 1929, led to a further increase in unemployment. The Prime Minister, J. Ramsay MacDonald, was so concerned about the country's financial position that he formed an all-party National Government in 1931. He split with Labour, his former party, in the process. The National Government's policy for recovery was to keep government spending to a minimum. The Labour party disagreed, saying that the Government should do the reverse and invest money in public works like roads, houses and schools to cure unemployment.

The unemployed were hit by the National Government's economy drive. In 1931, benefits for the insured were cut by ten per cent. The long-term unemployed 'on the dole' were now given a 'means test'. This meant that a man who had exhausted his stamps was turned over to the Public Assistance Committee which demanded details of his family's total income before deciding how much he needed. Even if his son had a three-shilling paper round or his wife had saved a few pounds in the post office, he had to declare these details and his 'dole' would be varied accordingly.

Needless to say, the means test was hated by the unemployed. It was, in Orwell's words, 'an encouragement to the tattle-tale and the informer'. If a child from a Public Assistance home was seen with a new coat or a bicycle, the 'means test man' would soon get to hear about it and call to inquire where it came from. The means test certainly saved the Government several million pounds a year, but the distress it caused was out of all proportion to its usefulness. Fathers were 'knocked off dole' altogether in some cases because their

53

sons and daughters had regular jobs. Nothing could be more damaging to a man's self-respect than to have to be supported by his children.

Unemployment did not reach its peak until the winter of 1932–33, when almost 3 million men were out of work. Of these, over 500,000 had gone more than a year without a job. In 1934 Parliament passed the twenty-first Unemployment Act within the space of fourteen years. Insurance, based on contributions, was completely separated from assistance ('the dole') and the ten per cent reduction in benefits, made in 1931, was restored. All the other unemployed, who had exhausted their right to benefits, came under an Unemployment Assistance Board. The U.A.B., which came into operation in 1936, had offices all over Britain, thus relieving the overworked labour exchanges. The amount of assistance paid still depended on a means test, much to the disgust of the unemployed, although it was made a little less severe.

In addition to money payments, the U.A.B. was responsible for the welfare of the unemployed. Training centres were established to prepare people for new jobs which gave them

Unemployed miner in Wigan —where 17 out of 40 pits were closed, 1939

more chance of finding work. Help was given to those who wanted to move to other areas of the country where there was fuller employment. Older men, with little chance of finding work, were often given allotments of land where they grew vegetables and fruit and reared poultry or rabbits for their own families. This was a wonderful release from boredom and worry, and many enjoyed it so much that they could be seen working from dawn to dusk.

The depressed districts were now called Special Areas by the Government. Attempts were made to encourage industries to move to the Special Areas, but they were mostly unsuccessful. Mass unemployment remained for the rest of the 1930s, although it eased a little in some places after about 1934. By this time it had existed for so long that it was accepted as normal. Many young men had reached their mid-twenties without ever having a job! Untold harm was done to them. They had got used to a way of life which was a poor preparation for regular work when it finally came. If you spend years having breakfast at ten or eleven o'clock and sitting around all day, perhaps in a billiard hall or on a park bench, you do not feel much like getting into a routine of clocking-in for work at 8 a.m. and doing eight or nine hours of disciplined work.

'The Jarrow Crusade'

Some of the unemployed devoted their time to demonstrations and marches, of which the most famous was the 'Jarrow Crusade' of 1936. Situated on the river Tyne, in County Durham, Jarrow had long depended for its livelihood on its shipyard. However, in the early 1930s the slump hit Jarrow and the shipyard was dismantled. Quiet descended over the town as the dole queues got longer and longer. By 1935 three-quarters of the men were out of work. In the following year, it was decided to organise a march to London in protest. Throughout the summer, funds were collected, a great banner was stitched and boots were repaired. On 5 October, 200 men, chosen from hundreds of volunteers, set off on the road to London, nearly 300 miles away. Jarrow's M.P., Ellen Wilkinson, led the way. The marchers took turns to carry a heavy oak chest containing a petition which was to

The Jarrow marchers, nearing London

be presented in Parliament to Stanley Baldwin, the Prime Minister.

On 1 November the marchers entered London, in a cloudburst, singing to their mouth organ band. They seemed like foreigners beside the better-dressed, better-fed people of the south-east. Next day, while the men sat in the public gallery of the House of Commons, Ellen Wilkinson presented the petition, containing 12,000 signatures. She said:

'During the last fifteen years, Jarrow has passed through a period of industrial depression unparalleled. . . . Its shipyard is closed. . . . Where formerly 8,000 persons, many of them skilled workmen, were employed, only a hundred are now employed on a temporary scheme. The town cannot be left derelict.'

A short debate followed. The Government was asked why it could not direct necessary Admiralty orders to Jarrow shipyards, but no answer was forthcoming. It was a disappointing anticlimax.

The marchers returned from King's Cross by special train. It was 5 November, and they were no doubt in sympathy with the intentions of the man who had made the day famous.

It seemed as though the whole of Jarrow was out to meet their arrival. The Unemployment Assistance Board provided the only sour note by deducting several shillings from the allowances of the marchers. It was explained that while they were away they had not been available for work if any had turned up. Nevertheless, despite the cool reception given them by the Government and the heartless behaviour of the U.A.B. officials, the effort of the marchers was not wasted. They had stirred the public conscience, and that was their real aim.

Gradually new industry came to Jarrow—a steelworks, engineering and ship-breaking, and by 1939 it was recovering. But the 'Jarrow Crusade' was not forgotten. It became a symbol of the years of depression and 'the army of the unemployed'. During the Second World War, 1939–45, detailed plans were made in the hope of preventing a recurrence of the misery and hardship of mass unemployment.

7 No 'Homes for Heroes'

Next to unemployment, housing was the greatest social problem in the 1920s and '30s. Rows of dismal terraced houses and crumbling cottages still disfigured both town and countryside —a large proportion of them without baths or inside lavatories. Worse still, there were not enough houses to go round, which caused great overcrowding in the poorer districts of the towns. After the Great War, workers and their families became increasingly dissatisfied with their living conditions. More and better houses were urgently required. Lloyd George raised everyone's hopes in 1918 when he spoke of 'homes fit for heroes to live in'. However, this promise, like many made after the war, could not be kept in the difficult times which lay ahead.

The housing shortage

House-building had always lagged behind the growth of population. Prewar Governments, including the Liberals, had done little to improve the situation. They were always reluctant to interfere with private property, unless it was a matter of public health. As a result, local authorities had been more concerned with knocking down bad houses than building better ones. War increased the shortage. Building stopped almost completely for four years while the country concentrated its manpower and resources upon the cause of victory. By 1918 there was a shortage of over half a million houses. This deficit would have to be made up before any programme of slum clearance could be contemplated.

Whenever things are scarce, they become more expensive and the people with the lowest incomes suffer. Housing is no exception. Even before 1914 it was impossible to build decent houses at rents the lower-paid workers could afford. They usually had to make do with a couple of rooms or a poky slum. After the war this problem increased, due to a rise in the cost of materials. It was not so bad for those who could afford to

58

Family living in one room in the East End of London, 1923

pay more; they still got what they wanted. The real shortage was of houses which were cheap enough for families with small incomes. As George Orwell said: '"Housing shortage" . . . means very little to anyone with an income of more than £10 a week, or even £5 a week for that matter.' The problem was not confined to the towns. Even in the countryside, much-needed cottages were not built because the rents that would have to be charged for them were beyond the means of farm labourers.

The attack on the housing shortage

Government intervention was the only answer, especially after Lloyd George's rash promise. A Housing Act (1919) at last recognised the fact that private builders could no longer build reasonable houses at low rents. Local authorities were therefore asked to find out how many extra houses they needed and submit plans for providing them to the new Ministry of Health, which was formed in the same year. The Government gave financial assistance in the form of sub-sidies (money grants) to avoid putting too great a burden on the ratepayers. Private builders could qualify for subsidies too, but only if they built houses suitable for families with small incomes.

By 1921 the demand for subsidies had become so great that the Government could not stand the cost. The 1919 plan was scrapped. If 'homes for heroes' were going to be so expensive the 'heroes' might have to go without! But the Government could not back out now. Besides, the shortage was increasing. Therefore subsidies were restarted but a limit was put on them. In 1924 the Government offered local authorities £9 a year for forty years on each new house they built to the required standard and let at a rent working-class families could afford. Rapid strides were made in the next ten years, before the subsidy was ended in the National Government's economy drive. Estates of 'council houses' appeared all over Britain. They were rather dull and plain perhaps, but they were far superior to previous working-class homes.

Nevertheless, the hope that the majority of new houses would be let at low rents was not fulfilled. The greatest expansion was still in the building of privately owned houses. 'Council houses' only accounted for a third of the total built in this period. Even then, in spite of subsidies, local authorities found it very difficult to keep rents low enough. Most of their houses went to the better-paid workers in safe jobs. The poor and the unemployed had to put up with what they had got. By the 1930s there were *more than enough* houses in the middle and upper price ranges. The shortage was now entirely confined to cheap, rented houses. George Orwell observed that in the poorer parts of the industrial towns, 'the mere difficulty of getting hold of a house . . . means that people will put up with anything—any hole and corner slum, any misery of bugs and rotting floors and cracking walls'.

Slum clearance

Until the 1930s slums were largely ignored by the Government. It would have been foolish to tear down existing houses, however bad they were, when there was a serious shortage. By 1930, however, the supply of houses had increased sufficiently for the Government to offer a special subsidy to local authorities for slum clearance. The aim was not just to pull

Typical working class houses in London, 1925—in need of demolition

slums down, as the Victorians·had done, but also to rehouse their inhabitants. To make sure of this, the subsidy was only paid if the slum dwellers were given houses at rents they 'could reasonably be expected to pay'.

In 1933, local authorities were asked to prepare complete programmes for the abolition of slums within five years. Despite great progress in many areas, however, only just over half of the work was done by 1939. Lingering on into the 1940s were conditions like these George Orwell found: 'You might walk ... through ... hundreds of miles of streets inhabited by miners, every one of whom, when he is in work, gets black from head to foot every day, without ever passing a house in which one could have a bath.'

Nevertheless, overcrowding was an even greater enemy of health and happiness. It was better to have no bath than to sleep three in a bed! It might have been more sensible if the Government had tried to get a separate dwelling for each family before it began to demolish the slums. Not until 1935 was serious overcrowding made illegal and a five-year plan to abolish it started. But it came too late. War interrupted, and bomb damage put the clock back several years.

Estate of smart, privately-owned houses in Birmingham, 1939

The great burst of house-building between 1919 and 1939 had rehoused almost half of the total population. Yet not enough of the right sort of houses were built. Over two-thirds were constructed by private builders, most of them for sale to families with comfortable incomes. By 1939 there were more houses than required for all but the poorest section of the population. Those who were not fortunate enough to get a council house continued to suffer dwellings without baths or inside toilets and often overcrowding as well.

Health insurance, pensions and local government

Throughout the 1920s and '30s, National Insurance against sickness remained firmly based on the original scheme of 1911. Rising prices caused the rates of contribution and benefit to be increased, and young workers aged fourteen to sixteen were brought into the scheme in 1937, but otherwise there were no important changes. Thus the wives and children of insured workers were still excluded from free medical attention.

To keep up with the cost of living, pensions were raised to 10s a week in 1919. With the proportion of elderly people in the community increasing every year, the cost of pensions to the Government was rapidly getting out of hand. Up to 1925 they cost the State more than any other social service, including unemployment benefits. As a result, a contributory scheme was introduced whereby people of working age paid a small weekly sum to offset the cost of their pension when they retired. At the same time, widows and orphans were included, for there was still no help except the poor law for families whose breadwinner had died. 'This is the greatest evil and the greatest need of the present time,' said Churchill, now a Conservative Chancellor of the Exchequer, in his 1925 budget speech.

The 1925 contributory pensions scheme was linked with health insurance. The same card was used to record both contributions. The Act which brought the scheme into force was based on the policy of the previous Labour Government. It was the work of Joseph Chamberlain's son Neville, the Conservative Minister of Health from 1924 to 1929. He was a skilful administrator, and the 1925 Act, which, he claimed, completed 'the circle of security for the worker', was only the start of his ambitious programme of reform.

However, the 'circle of security' was far from being complete, as was shown by the large numbers on poor relief in these years. Reform of the poor law was long overdue. Back in 1909 a Royal Commission had suggested that it should be abolished and its functions handed over to the local authorities. This was partly achieved by Chamberlain's Local Government Act of 1929. The Boards of Guardians were at last disbanded, and poor relief was renamed Public Assistance and taken over by the County and County Borough Councils. The cost of relief could now be spread over a wider area. At the same time, Urban and Rural District Councils were regrouped, leaving fewer, larger ones, and County Councils were given bigger grants and extra responsibilities for roads, town planning and child welfare.

Education and child welfare

When the war finished, expansion of State education was an essential part of Lloyd George's dream of a 'new Britain'. The President of the Board of Education, H. A. L. Fisher, regarded education as 'the most fundamental of all the social services', and, largely through his efforts, an Education Act of 1918 opened the way to future progress. The school leaving age was at last fixed at fourteen. It was hoped to continue part-time education beyond fourteen, but lack of money ruled this out almost from the start. Education grants to local authorities were cut by a third in 1921. For most young people, continued education after fourteen would have to be at 'night school'. In addition, the Act extended medical attention from the elementary to the secondary schools, and the employment of schoolchildren was restricted to little more than a newspaper round.

Secondary education expanded fairly rapidly after the Fisher Act. Meanwhile, the curriculum was gradually widened to include science, handicrafts and physical training. However, serious inequalities remained. In principle, it was widely believed that no child should be barred from educational opportunity just because its parents could not afford fees. But, in practice, it did not work out that way. Unless they were very clever, working-class children remained at elementary school until they left at fourteen. On the other hand, unless they were very stupid, children from more wealthy homes went to grammar school, or some other kind of fee-paying school, until they were sixteen or eighteen.

In 1926 a special committee under Sir Henry Hadow recommended secondary education for all, as a right not a

A primary school class, 1925

privilege. The Hadow Report criticised 'all age' schools. It suggested separate infant and junior schools, to be followed by either grammar or senior elementary schools, depending upon the 'different interests and abilities' of the pupils. Children would be transferred at eleven. '. . . not merely to a different type of teaching within the same school, but to another institution, with a distinctive staff, and organised definitely for post-primary education'. These proposals were widely accepted, and the reorganisation they suggested was about two-thirds completed by 1939. The Hadow Report also recommended a school leaving age of fifteen. After many delays, an Act bringing this about was prevented from coming into operation in September 1939 by the outbreak of the Second World War.

Ever since the school meals service started in 1906, it had been accepted that State education included more than just instruction. School medical services continued to play an important part in raising the general level of children's health. School meals, where provided, helped to relieve some of the strain of mass unemployment on children. However, even by 1939, less than half of all local education authorities provided solid meals. A Milk Act (1934) made it possible for children to have a third of a pint a day at the reduced price of $\frac{1}{2}d$, or free if they could not afford it.

Welfare services for children below school age were very uneven in distribution and quality. They still depended largely upon local initiative—either by go-ahead local authorities or by voluntary organisations. The demand for nurseries was especially great, now that more women than ever before were taking full-time jobs, but they remained in short supply. At the end of the 1930s, only about ten per cent of all children under five attended a nursery. There were two main kinds. Day nurseries took the children of working mothers and provided milk, meals and medical attention, and nursery schools and nursery classes in elementary schools were broadly educational in aim.

Perhaps the most important infant welfare service was provided by Health Visitors. They advised mothers of infants on ordinary day-to-day matters of health, hygiene and mothercraft. Despite a shortage of staff in many areas, ninety-seven per cent of all children born in England and Wales in 1938 were visited at least once. A similar function was performed by the Maternity and Child Welfare Clinics. They advised mothers on the feeding and general care of babies and young children and often provided extra services like vaccination, immunisation and the sale of cheap health foods. In 1938, seventy per cent of children born in that year attended a centre at least once. When the war came in 1939, priority was given to an immediate expansion of the welfare services for mothers and children.

8 Poverty and Progress in York, 1936

It is now time to return to the City of York and have another close look at working-class life through the eyes of Seebohm Rowntree. In 1936, Rowntree carried out a second survey of the living standards of York's lower-paid citizens. By comparing his findings with those of 1899, he hoped to measure roughly the extent to which people in a typical English city had benefited from over thirty years of State welfare services. As he rightly said, since his first investigation of 1899, 'more far-reaching steps had been taken to raise the standard of life of the workers than during any previous period of similar length.' At the same time, Rowntree hoped to underline the remaining causes of poverty and thus point the way to future social reforms.

Seebohm Rowntree

Below the poverty line

Every family whose chief wage-earner was paid less than £5 a week was investigated by one of seven interviewers. More than 55,000 people came into this category. To make a comparison with 1899 possible, a poverty line was calculated in the same way. After carefully considering the minimum amount of food, clothing and fuel necessary for the meanest existence, Rowntree arrived at a figure of 30s 7d, excluding rent, for a family of five. This was adjusted, as before, to fit different-sized families. It was a very bare standard of life, with nothing to spare for things like railway or bus fares, newspapers, letter-writing or smoking and drinking.

Rowntree found 3,767 people living below the poverty line —nearly four per cent of the total population, which was now about 90,000. He made no attempt to calculate the number of people who, although they had sufficient income, were in poverty through unwise spending. Therefore, the comparative figures from the two surveys in the table below only refer to what Rowntree called 'primary poverty'—people whose income was too low for the barest existence, even if they spent every penny wisely.

	1899	1936
Numbers in poverty	7,230	3,767
Percentage of total population in poverty	9·9	3·9

This was a great improvement in such a short space of time, but there was still much to be done. With one person out of every twenty-five in York still suffering terrible hardship, a great task lay before future reformers.

The investigation revealed some appalling details. One family of five, all out of work, was found to be living on bread and margarine alone for more than half of each week. This was in spite of unemployment assistance and a widow's pension. A girl of sixteen was prevented from getting work in a factory because she had no respectable clothing to wear. Most of the families in poverty had pawned or sold furniture to pay some of their debts. An old lady of seventy-two, living alone, had no bed and had to sleep on an old sofa. After paying her rent and buying a bag of coal, she had 3s 3d a week for all her other needs.

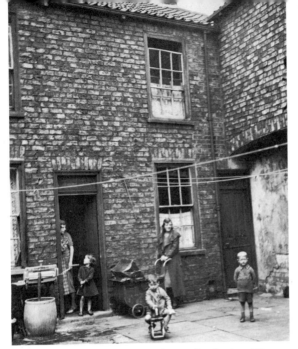
A York back-street in the 1930s—houses due for demolition

Causes of poverty

In 1899 more than half the poverty had been due to low wages. This was still a factor in 1936, but only in about one case in ten. The main cause of poverty now was long-term unemployment, which accounted for almost half of the total. Obviously the dole fell far short of what was needed. Temporary unemployment could usually be overcome by running up debts and by frequent visits to the pawnbroker, but when weeks turned into months, and months into years, deep poverty and a loss of self-confidence resulted. Rowntree disagreed with those who said the unemployed were lazy. He estimated that three-quarters of them were 'looking eagerly for work'.

Poverty in old age had also increased since 1899, in spite of retirement pensions. However, the proportion of old people in the community had nearly doubled since the turn of the century and they were now more independent. Many preferred to live alone in poverty rather than become a burden on their children, and very few even considered going into the workhouse. Nevertheless, the pension could hardly have been satisfactory since a fifth of the total in poverty were old people.

Even a married couple both drawing a pension required some extra form of income to raise them above the poverty line. Hardship in old age is especially distressing because there is so little chance of things ever getting better. Rowntree was very disturbed to find so many old folk 'pinching, scraping . . . just waiting for the end'.

The aged and the unemployed already received most of their income from the State. Therefore the way to raise them out of poverty was simply to increase existing rates of benefit and assistance. However, a more difficult problem was presented by large families which suffered poverty even though their fathers had regular jobs. The social services gave little or no help to these people. Rowntree, along with many other reformers, thought 'family allowances', based on the number of children in the family, should be paid by the State to overcome this kind of poverty. Wages were not related to family size, so it was possible for families above the poverty line to drop below it if additional children were born. Clearly, the time extra money was needed most was when the children were young. Rowntree showed that, apart from pensioners, young children had more chance of being in poverty than any other age-group—nearly half of all those in poverty in 1936 were under fourteen years of age.

In addition to family allowances, Rowntree again suggested a minimum wage as a way of removing poverty. On 1936 prices, it would have to be at least 53s: 'To keep a family of five in health on 53s a week . . . needs constant watchfulness and a high degree of skill on the part of the housewife.' He calculated that if a minimum wage of 53s and a family allowance of 5s for each child had been in operation in 1936, over ninety-eight per cent of the poverty among *families* would have been removed.

Housing, health and education

York City Council had taken great advantage of Government housing subsidies, having itself built more than half of all the new houses since 1920. As a result, the standard of workers' houses had greatly improved and there was much less overcrowding. Over a third of the working population now lived in comfortable, healthy houses—nearly all of them better

An early council estate in York

than the very best had been in 1899. Then, baths and gardens had been almost unknown in workers' houses, but now about a quarter had both. Although the number of slums had been halved, they still made up ten per cent of the total of houses. There was still a lot to do, but the end was in sight. Had it not been for the war, Rowntree estimated that 'the slum evil would practically have ceased to exist by 1945'.

Facilities for education compared favourably with those in other cities. As suggested by the Hadow Report, 1926, children went to primary schools until they were eleven, when they took examinations in English and Arithmetic to decide which kind of secondary school would suit them best. The highest secondary schools charged fees, but very poor parents did not have to pay. They could even get a maintenance allowance to help them keep their children at school beyond the leaving age. For those who left at fourteen, there was plenty of day continuation and evening education available. Even so, there was still much room for improvement. Classes of forty or fifty were common and many schools lacked changing and washing accommodation. Recreational facilities were poor, with only four playing fields available to 12,000 elementary school pupils.

On the whole, people were healthier than they had ever been. School clinics and free milk and meals for poor children were helping to produce a much stronger and fitter younger generation. Better food and improved sanitation helped to

71

prevent disease, so that the overall death rate had halved since 1899. The ill-fed, overworked people of 1899 had little energy for anything besides drinking. Now people lived a fuller life. Hours had been reduced from about fifty-four to between forty-four and forty-eight a week since the turn of the century. Holidays with pay were being introduced. With more leisure and better health, people now took part in a wide range of activities. York had swimming baths and sports clubs, dance halls, a theatre and a music hall. Even the most common entertainments, the cinema and wireless, had been unknown in 1899. For those who wanted to get out and about, there were cheap railway excursions, although many preferred cycling or, if they could afford it, motor-cycles and even cars.

There had certainly been an enormous improvement in the living standards of working people since 1899. Better wages and smaller families helped, but the main reason for the improvement was the growth of the social services. The workhouse, still important in 1899, was now almost empty. Nevertheless, to know that there had been twice as much poverty at the end of the nineteenth century hardly made that which remained any more tolerable for those who suffered it. As Rowntree said: 'If instead of looking backward we look forward, then we see how far the standard of living of many workers falls short of any standard which could be regarded as satisfactory.' Great progress had been made up to 1936, yet it will appear modest when compared with the rapid growth of social services during and after the Second World War.

PART THREE: 'FROM THE CRADLE TO THE GRAVE'

9 Evacuation

On 3 September 1939 Britain once again found herself at war with Germany. The six years of worldwide conflict which followed were to have a vitally important effect on the growth of the British Welfare State as we know it today. The Government was forced to reconsider the entire range of social services in the light of the strain put upon them by the war. Urgent reforms were found to be necessary. Some of them were carried out at once; others were included in the plans for postwar reconstruction. At the same time, a new sense of unity grew up among the people as they faced together the threat of invasion and conquest. They resolved to break for ever with the years of depression and succeed where their fathers had failed, in building a better Britain when peace returned.

The Second World War involved civilians just as much as the armed forces. The rapid advance of the aeroplane as a weapon of war meant that the bombing of enemy territory was now an important feature of military tactics. In these circumstances, the safety and welfare of the people at home had to be considered as well as the problem of providing enough soldiers and weapons. Plans were made in advance to move families away from areas close to probable air-raid targets into country districts where they would be much safer. The evacuation, as it was called, was the first stage in the 'war on the home front'.

A window on town life

The danger spots which were evacuated were mostly the dockland areas of the major ports, and the centres of vital war industries like munitions and aeroplane manufacture. Places like Glasgow, Liverpool and East London were thus affected. As it happened, these areas contained a large proportion of the remaining slums in Britain, so the evacuation provided a window through which the worst aspects of town life could be seen. During the first three days of September 1939 roughly a million and a quarter people were evacuated, most of them children. This was the main wave, although further movements brought the total of evacuees up to about 3 million by 1941.

Young children being evacuated from London to the West Country

Most of these people were clean and respectable, especially those from areas which had avoided the worst effects of unemployment. However, a less pleasant picture was presented by the evacuees from the slum districts, particularly the children. It was the end of the school holidays, and many of them had been running wild for over a month. Their arrival in the countryside, after a long, dirty train journey, was not, therefore, a very good advertisement for town living. Country hostesses had good cause to be shocked by the condition of some of the evacuees they received into their care.

The countryside itself was not free from poverty, but homes were generally much better, and dirty, ragged children much rarer. One of the first things to strike people in the reception areas was the appalling physical state of many of the evacuee children. Large numbers were infested with vermin, mainly head lice. These are flat, grey-white insects which lay whitish eggs, called 'nits', cemented to the hair near the roots. School medical services had long been fighting the problem of lice, and had largely stamped it out in the country areas, where it was now regarded as a disgrace. However, it was still the scourge of the poorer parts of industrial towns.

Head lice were especially common among girls and children under school age. The records of one clinic during the evacuation showed that two-thirds of one party of 320 London schoolchildren were infested with nits on arrival. Even after two or three years' evacuation, children were often re-infested if they visited their homes, and their heads had to be cleansed afresh on their return. Not only nits, but ringworm, impetigo, scabies and a host of other skin disorders were found. They were caused partly by bad housing conditions and lack of hygiene, and partly by ignorance. Some evacuee children and their parents claimed that lice were perfectly natural and saw no reason for alarm.

Needless to say, life in the slums had not encouraged the formation of good living habits. Many evacuee children were not used to a W.C. Even up to the age of fifteen, they thought nothing of relieving themselves in the street or on a sheet of newspaper. Country hostesses complained bitterly at having to wash clothes soiled through failure to use toilet paper and sheets fouled by frequent bed-wetting. Some of them had the greatest difficulty in getting children to wash themselves and despaired of trying to keep their clothing clean and tidy. Bad habits even extended to eating. Slum children often had no desire for wholesome food at regular meal-times. Instead, they clamoured for fish and chips, bread and jam, pickles, biscuits, sweets and ice cream.

'Evacuee stories' were soon spreading across garden fences and along shopping queues. The newspapers picked up some startling tales of dirt and neglect uncovered by the evacuation. They told of clothing which was so rotten it had to be cut off and burnt, or of children sewn into a single piece of calico, with a top coat as their only other clothing. Liverpool was nicknamed 'the plimsoll city' in the early months of the war because so many of its evacuated children had no proper outdoor shoes. Worse still, there were children without underwear, nightclothes or even a change of clothing of any kind. Some little girls had never worn knickers in their lives.

A turning point

The living conditions revealed by the evacuation came as a great surprise to the more fortunate section of the population. Many of them had assumed that, after more than thirty years of State social services, the 'Two Nations' had passed completely into the pages of history books. But the scar left by the depression was deeper and uglier than many thought possible. Some simply shook their heads disapprovingly at 'the way the other half lived', but, when the first shock had passed, an increasing number of people in all walks of life felt a burning sense of shame at the state of their society.

It was easy to blame parents for neglecting their children. Country folk were understandably annoyed at having to buy clothes for evacuee children while all their parents sent them was sweets and comics. However, the time had come to stop criticising and do something positive to raise the living standards of these people. The attempt to increase the supply of decent houses at low rents needed to be taken much further. Bad housing was a root cause of many of the evils revealed by the evacuation. It was almost impossible to train children in clean habits when houses, and even some schools, had no indoor lavatories, washing facilities or proper water supply.

One bad thing leads to another. Even sitting down to a family meal is unpleasant in a room several people have slept in. Children prefer fish and chips in the open air! Therefore regular eating habits are never formed, with an obvious effect on health. Noisy, damp and overcrowded slums, with bedbugs and irritating skin diseases to put up with, make sound sleep impossible. This, in turn, ruins both the health and the appetite and affects the mind as well as the body. Children go to school too tired to learn and adults are incapable of doing a good day's work. One little evacuee said of the country: 'I feel so well and happy here; I think it must be the lovely long sleeps we get.'

The remedies were not simple ones. Obviously a decent house for every family was the greatest need, together with an expanded, free health service. National insurance benefits would have to be increased. They had never been an adequate safeguard against poverty in times of hardship. It was not just a case of filling a few gaps in the existing social services; a whole new approach was necessary. Material help alone was not the answer. Education, in every sense of the word, was essential. People needed guidance and better standards held up to them. To put all these things right would require more far-reaching reforms than had ever been attempted before. However, in the spirit of wartime Britain, nothing seemed impossible.

By the summer of 1940, with invasion expected hourly, a new sense of social purpose arose in Britain. The war was a

City of London workers pick their way through rubble from destroyed buildings, 1940

great leveller. Never before had every man, woman and child
—rich and poor alike—at home or overseas—been so exposed
to the dangers of enemy attack. When German air-raids began
in August, continuing through the winter nights of 1940–41,
the people became even more united in their resolve to stand
together and resist. In response to the high-pitched whine of
the air-raid siren, they crowded together in communal shelters.
All of a sudden, people found they were not divided into
'classes' any more. Rich and poor alike were affected by
bomb damage, rationing and shortages, and conscription into
the armed forces.

Warfare and welfare

In May 1940 an all-party Coalition Government was formed
under Winston Churchill—as if to emphasise the growing
unity of the nation. Labour Party leaders worked alongside
Conservatives in the War Cabinet, and all the bitter political
struggles of the 1930s were forgotten for the time being in face
of a common foe. It seemed natural to expect the social
services to take second place when the 'emergency' came, but,
as the familiar props of everyday life collapsed, so increasingly

Mr and Mrs Winston Churchill inspect air-raid damage in London, 1940

the Government found itself forced to step in. Maintaining the morale of civilians 'on the home front' was an essential part of the war effort. After all, one of the main objects of air attack was to try to break the spirit of the people and bring them to the point of surrender.

During the evacuation, the Government had secretly distributed money to Directors of Education to help them deal with serious cases of neglect that came to their attention. Children in reception areas who needed medical care were given it free of charge. Soon help was needed on a much wider scale by families of dead servicemen, expectant mothers whose husbands were abroad, elderly people cut off from their relations, and the young children of women working in the essential industries. Those on fixed incomes, like pensioners, suffered greatly from a rapid rise in prices after the outbreak of war. The Government immediately introduced supplementary (extra) pensions for old people and widows in 1940. If they had insufficient to live on, they could now apply for extra allowances. Over a million pensioners took advantage of the scheme, showing the widespread need that existed.

Supplementary pensions were paid out of the funds of the Unemployment Assistance Board, which was renamed the Assistance Board, in keeping with its wider functions. The means test was eased so that assistance could be given to all who needed it—a further indication of the Government's new attitude. From now on, social services were to be available to all who had need of them, not just the poor. School milk and meals, vitamin foods and milk for infants, and a host of other services, were provided for the people as a whole. As well as distributing cash, where needed, the Assistance Board also provided home helps for the sick and elderly, when enough staff were available. Through helping bombed-out families and others in distress the Assistance Board did much to remove the memory of its earlier association with the hated means test. This was just the beginning of what was to amount to a social revolution in the next few years.

10 Sir William Beveridge

The social services had long been in a state of confusion. They had been assembled, one by one, without any definite plan in view. Frequent changes, as in the case of unemployment assistance between the wars, only complicated things further. There were different rates of benefit for the sick and the unemployed, even though their needs were the same; more than one contribution card was necessary, and a whole host of government departments were in charge of separate funds for similar purposes. The Coalition Government filled some serious gaps, but these emergency measures, however necessary they were at the time, only led to greater confusion in the long run. Small wonder that many people did not know whether they were entitled to any benefits or not.

It was clearly time to make a thorough investigation of 'social security' in particular, to see if a more logical and complete system could be planned. In June 1941, the Government ordered a special Committee of Inquiry to undertake ' a survey of the existing national schemes of social insurance . . . and to make recommendations'. The chairman of the committee was Sir William Beveridge. No one was better fitted for the

Sir William Beveridge—architect of the welfare state

task. He had a greater knowledge of social insurance than any other man of his time, and, through long experience, a rare grasp of the difficulties that faced ordinary people in their lives. He was given sole responsibility for settling the contents of the report and signing it, although he was to work with a team of eleven hand-picked civil servants, all experts in different fields.

Beveridge aimed to reconstruct social insurance so as to make all the parts interlock, like the pieces of a jigsaw puzzle. Only by fitting everything into a single plan could the gaps be eliminated and overlapping be avoided. There could be no better time for making a fresh start. As Beveridge said: 'Now, when war is abolishing landmarks of every kind, is the opportunity of using experience in a clear field. A revolutionary moment in the world's history is a time for revolutions, not for patching.' All interested bodies were consulted, including the trade unions, friendly societies and several industrial insurance companies. In all, over forty sets of witnesses were called. Even recent social surveys, including Rowntree's investigation of 1936, were carefully considered. At the end of 1942 the Report was ready. Despite its length (200,000 words, or nearly six times longer than this book) and its complicated calculations, the basic proposals were few, simple and clear.

The Beveridge Report

Beveridge proposed a complete system of insurance covering *all* citizens, whatever their income. Everyone of working age would pay a single weekly contribution, recorded by a stamp on a single card. Employers would continue to pay part of the cost of their employees' stamps. Men would need to pay more than working women, for housewives were to be covered by their husbands' insurance.

In return for contributions, flat rate benefits would be paid to all citizens on 'interruption of earnings'—sickness, unemployment or retirement. There would be no time limit on benefits, 'they will continue indefinitely . . . as long as the need continues'. The actual weekly rates would depend on a calculation of the minimum income necessary. Thus benefits were to be based on a 'national minimum'—a standard of decent living below which no one should for any reason be allowed to fall. In addition, there would be extra grants for the normal incidents of life which demanded extra expenditure—maternity grants on the birth of children, and a funeral grant.

This was the basis of Beveridge's suggested replacement for all the bits and pieces of insurance and pensions that had grown up since 1908. It was a simple redistribution of income, achieved by a 'pooling of risks' of the whole community. No means test would be necessary. All citizens would be equal members of the scheme, with an equal right to draw benefits. Beveridge suggested a single new Ministry of Social Security to organise the plan—a great simplification of the arrangements then in force. Because the whole plan was firmly based on the principle of insurance, the State would not be involved in enormous expense. However, the Government would be expected to stand the full cost of family allowances. These were to be paid weekly to parents for each dependent child. Beveridge said they were essential because wages were never related to the needs of a growing family.

The insurance scheme was not a complete system of social security. It dealt only with *want*, and, as Beveridge said, 'Want is only one of the five giants on the road of reconstruction and social progress.' The other 'giants' were *disease*, which would require a new health service, 'securing medical treatment of all kinds for all citizens'; *ignorance*, which could only be overcome with 'more and better schools'; *squalor*, which meant 'more and better houses' so that every family had a decent home, and *idleness*, or unemployment. This could only be kept in check by tighter government control of trade and industry. Beveridge said that if the Government had concentrated on making sure there was enough work, they would not have had to patch the holes in insurance with 'doles' in the years between the wars.

The Beveridge Report was the most important single influence on the making of the Welfare State. Although the method of approach was original, most of the contents were already familiar. Apart from family allowances and the death grant, and the principles of applying insurance to everyone, no matter what their income might be, the plan was firmly based on the foundations of 1911. It simply rounded off all that had gone before. As Beveridge said: 'The scheme proposed is in some ways a revolution, but in more important ways it is a natural development from the past.'

Public approval

On 2 December 1942 the newspapers set out the details of the finished plan. It was immediately received by the public like a new gospel. Long queues formed outside His Majesty's Stationery Office, where the Report was on sale. Official

literature had never been so eagerly read. The Report was a best seller from the start, and before long well over half a million copies were sold. Beveridge had succeeded in capturing the spirit of the times, and he became a national hero overnight. As an American commentator put it: 'Sir William, possibly next to Mr Churchill, is the most popular figure in Britain today.'

Soldiers overseas were equally eager to get information about the Report. The plan for the abolition of want gave them something to fight *for* as well as against. Beveridge was well aware of this need. He said of his proposals: 'They are a sign of the belief that the object of government in peace and in war is not the glory of rulers or of races, but the happiness of the common man.' The Army Bureau of Current Affairs produced a pamphlet on the Beveridge plan for distribution among soldiers. Even the Americans wanted to read about it. The Treasury made a profit of $5,000 from sales of a special American edition of the Report.

As with all plans for reform, there was criticism of the Report. Some dismissed it as being too ambitious. Others were disturbed by the fear that it gave *too much* security, so that people would no longer have to 'save for a rainy day'. The most common criticism was that the inclusion of all citizens in the insurance scheme and family allowances would mean that well-to-do people would draw benefits they did not need. But most people realised that this was, in fact, one of the strengths of the plan. Everyone had a legal right to claim benefit, so there was no need for a means test and no suggestion of poor relief about it. The principle of a 'national minimum' standard of living would at last be achieved. This was probably the most attractive feature of the whole Report.

The critics were in a small minority. By and large, there was overwhelming agreement that the Beveridge plan should be put into effect. 'Social security from the cradle to the grave'—this was the new Britain that people wanted. Beveridge himself was left in no doubt about the public reception of his Report. He was approached in the street by people who wished to thank him personally. An old age pensioner from Plymouth sent him thanks in the form of a verse:

> At last there is a saint on earth;
> An angel he would be
> If only he could have his will
> And make the Commons pass his bill.

Government caution

As the pensioner's verse indicated, there was not yet any promise from the Government that the Report would become law. True, they had asked Beveridge to undertake the task, but he was only asked to make 'recommendations'. Whether the recommendations were acted upon was quite another matter. Beveridge was well aware of the position, and, in a broadcast, he warned people not to take the Government's attitude for granted:

'What I have been telling you is simply my proposals to the Government. The Government are not committed in any way to anything that I have said. They've only just seen my Report and you won't expect them to make up their minds . . . without full consideration.'

In fact, Churchill's Cabinet was in a difficult position. They thought they had ordered a technical survey of social insurance which could be used as a basis for reform but did not commit

Beveridge during a campaign of speeches, 1943. (He was not a great speaker, but at this time he could fill any hall in Britain)

them in any way. Instead they were presented with a fully-fledged programme of reform, carefully worked out to the last letter. The great publicity it was given and the great public

85

acclaim it received embarrassed the Government still further. It seemed that they were the only people in Britain who had not made up their minds about the Report. After the failure of all the bright promises of 1918 about 'a land fit for heroes', they were particularly anxious not to raise false hopes this time. Therefore they delayed making definite plans until they had taken a long, careful look at the Report.

The Beveridge Plan was debated in the Commons for three days in February 1943, but the Government refrained from making any promises. A government spokesman said it was 'bold and imaginative' and that the financial situation at the end of the war would determine what could be done. A motion in favour of the Report was carried by 335 votes to 119 and there things rested for a while. In the following month, Churchill, in a broadcast, promised a four-year plan of reconstruction after the war but, at the same time, warned against too much talk of peace while the war was still raging. He did not think it was fair to tell 'fairy stories' about the future. Meanwhile, the Beveridge Report was being considered by a committee of officials in Whitehall. Eventually, in 1944, a new scheme of social insurance was prepared. It was firmly based on Beveridge's plan, although one or two important adjustments were made—as you will see when we come to National Insurance.

11 Child Welfare and Education

In the darkest years of the war, before the Beveridge Report became the centre of attention, great advances were made in the care of children. From the evacuation, which revealed so much neglect, right through the heavy bombing of 1940–41, the needs of the young always came first. The Government did all in its power to combat ill health and undernourishment among children—'the raw material of the race'. Not only physical needs were met. Before the war was over, the entire system of education was reformed in the Act of 1944, which established the pattern of State education for almost a quarter of a century.

Infant welfare

One of the most disturbing things brought to light by the evacuation was the poor physical condition of many children below school age. They were the worst affected by nits and other marks of bad living conditions. It was clearly absurd to allow the health of a child to deteriorate until it was five and then spend the next ten years, through the school medical service, trying to put right disorders which could have been prevented. The Government therefore decided to give top priority to the nourishment and medical care of infants and their mothers. But they no longer thought in terms of poor relief. The shortages, mishaps and dangers of war were shared by the whole population, and it was the Government's duty to protect the health and well-being of every child, rich or poor.

A National Milk Scheme was started in July 1940. All children under five and expectant and nursing mothers were entitled to a pint of milk a day for twopence, instead of the full price of 4½d. If the family income was below £2 a week, the milk was given free. National Dried Milk for babies was soon offered as an alternative. The entire cost of the subsidy

87

was met by the Government, for, as Churchill said: 'There is no finer investment for any community than putting milk into babies.' Since this was a genuine social service, available to everyone, it was enormously popular. By the end of the war there were nearly 4 million consumers of subsidised milk, and the scheme was continued in peacetime.

By 1941 the effects of the war on foreign trade were causing concern about the nation's diet. Imported fruits like oranges had almost disappeared from the shops, and there was a danger that expectant mothers and young children might suffer from a deficiency of vitamin C. The Ministry of Health acted quickly. Cod-liver oil and blackcurrant extracts were made available, free of charge, at welfare centres and food offices. Early in 1942 National Rose Hip Syrup, a valuable source of vitamin C, appeared in chemists' shops, reserved mainly for young children. This was produced in large quantities as a result of a remarkable campaign. Throughout the summer and autumn of 1941, women's and children's organisations, including the Scouts and Girl Guides, scoured the hedgerows for rose hips. They picked about 200 tons in all —enough to employ nine firms with the job of making the syrup.

Before long concentrated orange juice began to be obtained

A child receiving essential foods from the 'Hand of war'

from the U.S.A., and this gradually replaced the blackcurrant products. The milk and vitamin food schemes had already been merged, and a small charge was put on the vitamin foods. By the end of 1942 all children under five and expectant mothers were supplied with subsidised milk, cod-liver oil and orange juice. In November, the *Daily Mirror* said: 'Now here surely is a fact to give the utmost encouragement and hope to all of us. In the midst of war, Great Britain is able to build better children's bodies than in times of peace.'

After the war, when fresh fruit and other sources of vitamins reappeared on the market, the scheme was not so essential. Nevertheless, when family allowances were introduced (1946) milk and vitamin foods were continued as part of the weekly benefits and renamed the Welfare Foods Service. Even today free welfare milk and vitamins are available to expectant mothers and children under five in families whose income is below a certain level. This is part of the Family Income Supplement scheme which started in 1971 (see p. 129).

When regular night bombing began, in the autumn of 1940, people were forced to crowd together into air-raid shelters. In these conditions, all kinds of infection could be passed on, not least among them diphtheria—the most dangerous of children's diseases. Before the end of the year, therefore, the Ministry of Health began a campaign to have children immunised against diphtheria. Leaflets, posters and advertisements in newspapers and magazines all warned parents of the danger. By the end of the war, half the nation's children had been immunised and no serious epidemic had occurred. The following figures tell their own story:

Deaths from diphtheria in Britain: 1938 nearly 3,000; 1945 about 720.

In contrast, deaths from the disease mounted in most other European countries during the war—especially in Germany.

The war put a great strain on the existing infant welfare services, especially in the evacuation areas. At first, many welfare centres had their buildings taken over by Civil Defence, and Health Visitors were often needed for other tasks. But gradually extra staff and buildings were found and the number of welfare centres actually increased by the end of the war. Voluntary workers played a very important part in

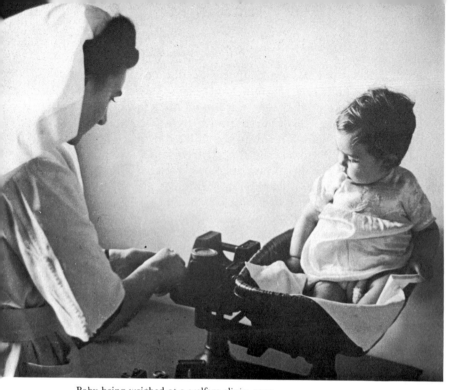

Baby being weighed at a welfare clinic, 1944

these services and also in the much needed expansion of
nurseries. The Government was eager to increase the intake
of married women into the essential industries. Therefore some
local authorities were given extra financial help to provide
more nurseries. As a result, more children were taught, where
necessary, good eating and sleeping habits and bodily cleanliness—things which had been found seriously lacking in many
evacuee children.

School milk and meals

Before July 1940 school meals had been little more than a
form of poor relief, to be provided for very undernourished
children. But the war brought about a complete change of
policy. With many mothers working, there was a great need
for midday school meals for children from all kinds of homes,
not just the poor. In any case, the Government was concerned
with the possible effect of food shortages on children's health,
and wanted to ensure that they all got a good meal at midday.

Children serving their own school dinners

Local Education Authorities were therefore encouraged to extend their meals service. An official report said: 'There is no question of capacity to pay. We may find children of well-to-do parents and the children of the poor suffering alike from an inability to get the food they need.'

After a year, the number of subsidised school meals being provided had doubled. The same attitude was taken over school milk—there was a fifty per cent increase in milk consumption during the same period. In September 1941, it was decided to provide milk for *all* schoolchildren at a subsidised price, although the poor continued to get theirs free. A year later, the *Daily Mirror* commented: 'Not so long ago hundreds of thousands of children of the poor never drank fresh milk. Now each child has at least half a pint a day.'

There could be no going back on this great advance when the war ended. Until 1968 a third of a pint of milk was given to all children free of charge. Similarly, meals at subsidised prices were made available to all who wanted them, and were free in cases of special need. By 1948 well over half

Mid-morning milk break

of all the pupils in State schools had their midday meal at school. Parents had no hesitation about using a service which was freely available to everyone, regardless of income.

Education and the 1944 Act

Throughout the war years, educational reform was one of the favourite topics of discussion. The future of Britain's schools was bound to be an important part of the plans for reconstruction. Broadcasting to the nation in 1943, Churchill stressed the importance of giving every child the fullest opportunity for development: 'We must make sure that the path to the highest functions throughout our society and empire is really open to the children of every family.'

The urgent demand for skilled workers during the war had revealed serious gaps in the education system—especially the sorry state of technical education. Churchill reminded the people that the future of the world was in the hands of 'the highly-educated races, who alone can handle the scientific apparatus necessary for pre-eminence in peace or survival in war. . . . You cannot conduct a modern community except with an adequate supply of persons upon whose education much time and money have been spent.'

In 1944, under the guidance of R. A. Butler, President of the Board of Education, a new Act brought together all the plans for educational reform in England and Wales. (The Scottish system had always developed independently and required separate Acts of Parliament.) 'Free secondary education for all' would be the basis of the postwar system. The reorganisation suggested by the Hadow Report (1926) was to be completed, with some important additions. The idea of 'elementary' education disappeared completely and was replaced by three progressive stages—primary, secondary and 'further'; and nursery schools would be provided for younger children. The leaving age was to be raised to fifteen almost immediately, and to sixteen as soon as possible. Physically and mentally handicapped children were not left out. It was the duty of Local Education Authorities to provide suitable schools for all children, according to 'age, aptitude and ability'—and milk, meals and medical and dental services as well.

In future, all children would leave primary school at 'eleven plus'. Those who were successful in an examination would proceed either to a grammar school, with an academic curriculum, or, where provided, to a technical school. The remainder would go to a 'modern' school, where the emphasis would be on practical subjects. It was intended to provide three years of part-time further education for fifteen-year-old leavers at 'county colleges'. A great expansion of universities and colleges of advanced technology (C.A.T.s) was also planned. Local authority grants for full-time study would make it possible for any boy or girl with sufficient ability to progress from school to university without financial help from their parents.

The 1944 Act in practice

All was ready for a massive expansion of secondary and further education when the war finished. However, there were many obstacles in the path of progress. Air-raids had destroyed or damaged 5,000 schools. This, together with the wartime rise in the birth rate, caused great overcrowding of existing buildings. Difficulties increased when the Government went ahead with the plan to raise the leaving age to fifteen in 1947. There were not enough teachers to cope with all the extra classes. An emergency campaign was started to attract people from all walks of life into special teacher-training courses. Throughout the summer of 1947 posters appealed to people to MAKE TEACHING YOUR CAREER. Meanwhile children were moving into new schools while bricklayers, carpenters and painters worked around them.

There was a limited amount of money available for education. The vast expenditure on the schools meant that the plan for county colleges was pushed into the background. Nevertheless, 'day release' classes at colleges of further education and technical colleges expanded rapidly, giving young people a chance to improve their qualifications while they were in a regular job. The shortage of teachers and buildings still seemed never-ending ten or twenty years after the war. It was not until 1964 that the Government went ahead with plans to raise the leaving age to sixteen. Even then it is not planned to come into operation until 1973.

Before long the system of selection at 'eleven plus' became the object of mounting criticism. People said it was unfair to make drastic decisions about a child's future at such an early age. Children often suffered from strain as a result of being 'crammed' for the examination, and in any case there were grave doubts whether the examination itself was sufficiently reliable. Newspapers began to carry stories of 'eleven plus failures' obtaining university degrees. All three types of secondary school were supposed to be equal in prestige, but this was just wishful thinking. The grammar schools had inherited a great reputation from their earlier days and they became the main objective of both parents and children, especially as they provided the surest route to higher education and the better-paid jobs. Instead of 'deciding suitability for different types of secondary education', the 'eleven plus' examination was a simple case of pass or fail—the 'sheep' to the grammar school; the 'goats' to the modern.

The 1944 Act did, however, go a long way towards removing wealth as a direct influence on State secondary education. With the exception of 165 'direct grant' grammar schools, which could still charge fees for half their places, the Act abolished fee-paying in grammar schools. Well-to-do families had previously been able to take a grammar school education almost for granted; for about half of them had charged fees before the war. Now, it was 'ordeal by eleven plus' for almost everyone. For this reason, private fee-paying schools, outside the State system, continued to flourish. Wealthy parents often sent their children to private schools if they 'failed' the 'eleven plus'. There they would be able to stay on until at least sixteen and take the new General Certificate of Education (G.C.E.), which replaced the School Certificate in 1951, even if it was only intended for 'academic' children who passed the 'eleven plus'.

Some local authorities had doubts about the 'eleven plus' right from the start. Even as the 1944 Act was becoming law, the London County Council voted in favour of 'comprehensive' schools. These would take children of all abilities at eleven and provide suitable courses for them under one roof,

Kidbrooke Comprehensive School

without the need for sending them to separate types of school. Primary schools had, of course, always been 'comprehensive'. When London County Council's first brand new secondary comprehensive school—Kidbrooke—was opened in 1954, with room for 1,700 girls and ninety staff, the newspaper headlines gave a clear indication of the great difference of opinion about this type of school. The *News Chronicle*, which has since ceased publication, hailed it as THE FIRST PALACE OF LEARNING, but the *Evening Standard* called it a SAUSAGE MACHINE!

As time went by, many local authorities modified the 'eleven plus' or scrapped it altogether. Modern schools began to develop extended courses to sixteen, often ending with the G.C.E.—a policy which was approved by the Government in 1958. The introduction of the Certificate of Secondary Education (C.S.E.) in 1965 was a recognition of the change that had come over the modern schools, for the C.S.E. was to be taken at the age of sixteen. By this time, some schools had dropped the label 'modern' altogether and become 'high schools'.

Leicestershire and Croydon had pioneered new schemes of two-stage secondary comprehensives, in an attempt to make use of existing buildings while doing away with selection at 'eleven plus'. Although only about one child in fifteen went to a comprehensive school in the early 1960s, the proportion was steadily increasing. Comprehensive schools were coming in 'by the back door' long before they were made the official policy of the Labour Government in 1965. From then on ambitious schemes of 'secondary reorganisation' began, often involving the amalgamation of former grammar and modern schools into single units.

The Children Act, 1948

The great advances in child welfare, which were either planned or already in operation by 1945, were, of course, primarily intended for children living with their families at home. However, an incident at the end of the war brought sharply into focus the needs of children deprived of a normal home life. A little boy called Denis O'Neill, who was boarded-out on a lonely farm in northern England, was thrashed so brutally that he died. This was not the first case of its kind by any means, yet public opinion was aroused as never before.

A special committee investigated local authorities' arrangements for taking children into care, and revealed some serious shortcomings. In some dreary 'institutions', normal children were found sleeping with mental defectives, and some of them were looked after by old people or cleaners! The resulting Children Act (1948) stressed the importance of a family background for deprived children, but made local authorities supervise 'boarding-out' much more strictly than before, to prevent any repeat of the Denis O'Neill incident. Children's Officers would find homes for deprived children and visit them regularly. All homes had to conform with standards laid down by the Home Office. Voluntary organisations, like the National Society for the Prevention of Cruelty to Children (N.S.P.C.C.) and Dr Barnardo's Homes, continued to flourish in co-operation with the State.

12 Social Security
—The Attack on Want

Germany surrendered on 7 May 1945, and Japan three months later, bringing the Second World War to an end. Peace had come at last, and with it the chance to build the 'new Britain' which had been planned so thoroughly during the war. Much had been done already. Infant welfare services and school milk and meals were well established, and the 1944 Education Act had begun the attack on the first of Beveridge's 'five giants'—Ignorance. Before the remaining 'giants' could be tackled, however, there would have to be a General Election, the first for ten years, to decide which party was to be entrusted with the task of reconstruction.

'The Labour landslide'

The Coalition Government was broken up in May 1945, having accomplished its task of bringing the war to a successful conclusion. For the next few months, Churchill and the Conservatives remained in office until an election could be held. Churchill had ambitious plans of his own for tackling the problems of reconstruction, including a great housing drive—to be planned like a military operation. Most people expected his great war record to carry him to victory at the polls. Imagine the surprise when, on 26 July, the following result was announced: Labour—393 seats; Conservative—198; Liberal and Independent—32. The Labour victory was even more decisive than that of the Liberals in 1905! Like the result forty years before, the 1945 election heralded a period of great reforming activity.

The election result was not intended to be a rejection of Churchill's great achievements as a war leader. He was a national hero, and remains so. When he died in 1965 he was honoured as no Englishman had ever been before. It was simply that people wanted to break with the past—the days of 'dole' queues and the means test. Labour had been in power

98

for less than three years throughout the whole of the 1920s and '30s, so they were relatively free from blame for the years of depression. A Conservative M.P., Christopher Hollis, later said of the election result: 'However we may have voted in 1945, none of us looking back can deny there was at that time a general feeling of disgust in the nation, just or unjust, with the past.'

The new Prime Minister, Clement Attlee, and his Cabinet, had a mammoth task before them. Britain's finances had been shattered by vast war expenditure, and large areas of several major towns and cities had been reduced to rubble in the air-raids. Food, clothing and fuel were strictly rationed, and almost everything was in short supply. There could hardly have been a more difficult time for the Government to take on all the extra responsibility necessary for the creation of a Welfare State. But the people were determined that nothing should be allowed to hold back the tide of social reform. 1945 was not a time for excuses or delay.

Family allowances

The heart of the Beveridge plan was 'social security'—the attack on Want. This would be achieved in the main by National Insurance, but family allowances were an important part of the overall scheme. They had already become law in 1945, before the election, although the first payments were not made until August 1946. The arguments in favour of family allowances put forward by Beveridge, Rowntree and a host of others before them, had proved unanswerable. Because an unskilled workman's wages reached their peak in early manhood, each time his wife had a child the standard of living of the whole family was lowered. Since the idea of a national minimum wage had failed to gain acceptance, family allowances were the next best thing. They ensured that extra money went *at the right time* to those who needed it.

Beveridge had suggested a weekly allowance of 8*s* for each child, but the Act fixed it at 5*s* for each child *after the first*, up to the age of sixteen or the start of full-time employment. It was given in the form of a book of coupons, to be cashed at a post office. The Government justified the smaller sum of 5*s* on the grounds that welfare foods and school milk and meals had been expanded to a far greater extent than Beveridge could have foreseen. By shifting some of the allowance on to these services, the child was ensured of getting some of the benefit directly. Allowances were not given for the first child because it was assumed that the family income would be sufficient to stand the cost of one child without hardship. The State did not intend to take over the responsibility of parents for their children. Allowances did not cover all the cost of a child's upbringing—the financial burden was shared between the parents and the community as a whole.

Family allowances were not based on insurance contributions, therefore the entire cost came out of national taxation. Any family could qualify for them, regardless of income. This was criticised, on the grounds that most families could manage without the extra money. However, the basic principle of the new social services was that they should avoid the need for means tests as far as possible. Thus every family was treated alike; although, in practice, the poorest ones gained most from family allowances because they did not have to pay income tax on them. The rates of allowances were increased in 1952, 1956 (when third and additional children received more than the second, and the age limit was raised to eighteen for children in full time education) and again in 1968. At the time of the last rise the Government introduced a 'clawback' arrangement, whereby the whole of the increase was taken back from better-off families by adjusting the father's income tax payments.

National Insurance

After some delay, the Coalition Government accepted most of Beveridge's proposals in 1944, and a new Ministry of National Insurance was set up. The Labour Government carried on with the wartime plans, and National Insurance became law in 1946. The Act differed from the Beveridge Report in one very important respect. It was not based on a 'national minimum' standard of living. This would have required automatic adjustments to meet changes in the cost of living, and the Government thought this was too complicated. They preferred to fix rates of benefit which would be a reasonable insurance against want and review them at five-year intervals.

In fact, with the rapid rise in prices, benefits soon fell a long way behind minimum needs. Further Acts were necessary, at much more frequent intervals than intended, to bring contributions and benefits in line with the cost of living.

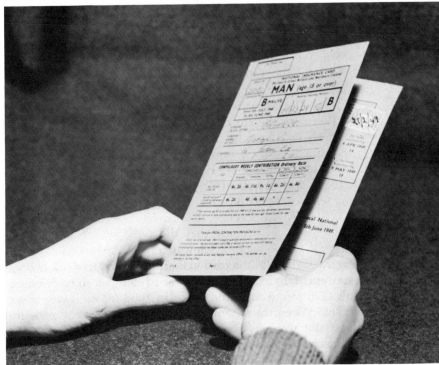

A National Insurance Card

National Insurance was compulsory for everyone of working age except married women. Rates of contribution varied according to whether people were employed, self-employed or unemployed. Lower scales of contribution and benefit applied to boys and girls under eighteen. Benefits were paid for 'interruption of earnings', caused by sickness, unemployment or old age. However, if earnings were lost through taking part in a strike, benefit was not paid. It was up to the trade unions to provide their members with 'strike pay'. Benefits could also be postponed if claimants refused to take any suitable job that was offered them by the labour exchange. Pensions were paid

A new employment exchange, 1949. (Notice the padded chairs and comfortable benches for those awaiting interview)

on 'retirement'. Old people were encouraged to work beyond the normal retiring age of sixty-five (men) or sixty (women) by an addition to the basic rate of pension for each year it was deferred. When the scheme began, two-thirds of the men and half of the women who qualified for a pension decided to continue working.

In addition, there were a host of other benefits stemming from the weekly contribution. Maternity grants were given to mothers—a lump sum paid on the birth of each child. If the mother had previously been working and had paid enough contributions, she got an additional allowance for eighteen weeks from her own insurance. Then there was the death grant, to help with funeral expenses, and widows' pensions and guardians' allowances. A separate, but linked, scheme was introduced by the Industrial Injuries Act (1946). It dealt with compensation for those injured, disabled or killed at work, and those suffering from industrial diseases.

Needless to say, for all the benefits offered, weekly contributions had to be fairly substantial. The rate for employed persons was 4*s* 11*d* when the scheme started. Although this was a considerable sum, it was in fact less than the cost of all the separate schemes before they were combined. The Government still had to make a large additional contribution on top of this. James Griffiths, Minister of National Insurance, said the scheme was 'the best and the cheapest insurance policy offered to the British people, or to any people anywhere'. Speaking for the Opposition in Parliament, R. A. Butler said: 'I think we should take pride that the British race has been able . . . shortly after the terrible period through which we have all passed together, to show the whole world that we are able to produce a social insurance scheme of this character.'

The running of the scheme was a vast undertaking. The records of every insured person were kept in the central offices of the Ministry of National Insurance, which were built on the outskirts of Newcastle. *The Times* explained some of the workings of the system: 'Each insured person has his own ledger-sheet on which his whole insurance life history can be recorded; and there are similar records for the family allowance scheme. The 25,000,000 sheets of the insurance ledger are located in 100 different rooms, each of which is occupied by a staff of twenty.' Everyone had an insurance number. This was simpler than using names, especially if the name was Smith. There were 650,000 members of the Smith family in the scheme—8,000 of them plain John Smith!

The insurance scheme which began in 1948 remains the basis of the present system of social security. Nevertheless, there has been an important change of principle in recent years. By the late-1950s, most people's earnings had increased to such an extent that there was an enormous gap between their regular income and National Insurance benefits. This was particularly serious in the case of pensions—for example, a workman, who was now likely to be earning £15 to £20 a week, dropped *permanently* to about £4 when he retired. As a consequence, many employers were running *additional* private pensions schemes, and these covered nearly half of all employed men by 1958. The time seemed ripe to extend National Insurance pensions, so that both contributions and benefits could somehow be related to the normal income of each employee. The resulting scheme of Graduated Pensions began in April 1961.

Employees who earned over £9 and did not belong to a satisfactory private scheme paid a little extra each week for a larger pension on retirement.

From October 1966, the same principle was applied to sickness and unemployment benefit and widows' pensions. These were now related to normal earnings, in return for an additional graduated contribution ranging from 1d per week from those earning just over £9, to 2s 1d from those earning £30 or more. Benefits were only payable from the start of the third week of 'interruption of earnings' and then only for twenty-six weeks at a time, but they were substantially increased. For example, if a married man with one child earned £18 a week he received £10 12s 6d instead of the old flat rate of £7 12s 6d. If he earned £30 or more, he qualified for the maximum benefit of £14 12s 6d.

National Assistance

Not all citizens are normally healthy or reasonably fortunate. Some people need looking after even though they have not paid for the right through insurance. They include the blind, deaf, crippled, insane, deserted or unmarried mothers and the wives and children of criminals. The National Assistance Board was established in 1948 to take over responsibility for these people. It was the disguised descendant of the poor law. The cost of poor relief, which had once fallen on the parish, was now, through national taxation, spread over the whole nation. Three hundred and fifty years of social history, going back to the Elizabethan Poor Law of 1598, had been neatly rounded off. Among its many duties, the Assistance Board had to provide Reception and Re-establishment Centres for the homeless, where they could be trained for re-entry into employment; and old people's homes, run by local authorities.

In addition, the Assistance Board was to provide a 'safety net' for those whose needs were not fully satisfied by National Insurance benefits. It was hoped that it would not have an active future in this respect, but the reverse happened in practice. The failure to base insurance benefits on a minimum standard of living meant that the 'safety net' was soon bulging. Most of the 'casualties' were old people, who found that the pension was not enough to live on. Beveridge himself pointed out with regret, in 1953, that a quarter of all those receiving

An applicant for National Assistance undergoing a 'needs test'

retirement or widows' pensions had to go to the Assistance Board for extra help. The proportion would have been higher still if everyone in need had applied. However, many old people were too proud to ask for what they regarded as charity.

National Assistance was available to anyone over sixteen who could show he was in need of help. It was therefore necessary for applicants to undergo a 'needs test'. This was not like the old means test, however, because the incomes of the other members of the family did not have to be declared. The whole service was very personal. Each case was different and was treated on its merits. The Board could give weekly cash donations, lump sums for things like tools for a job, and even allowances of clothing or bedding, if needed. The Board's calculations were based on certain minimum standards of living (like Rowntree's 'poverty line', except that they were a little more generous). Therefore the 'national minimum' idea was not entirely lost. The Assistance Board merged with the Ministry of National Insurance in 1966 and the duties of both were taken over by a unified Ministry of Social Security. This, in turn, merged with the Health Ministry in 1968 to form the *Department of Health and Social Security*.

Full employment

Beveridge had warned that his whole scheme of social security could break down if mass unemployment—the 'giant Idleness'—continued after the war. He urged the Government to take on much greater responsibility for maintaining a high level of employment. This would mean keeping tight control over things like the distribution of industry and labour, and the retraining of redundant workers for new jobs. Industrial 'slumps' caused too much suffering to be allowed to correct themselves, as had been the practice in the past.

There were still a million unemployed in 1940, but the wartime emergency eventually occupied idle hands. By 1943 the figure dropped as low as 100,000 for a time. Nevertheless, circumstances were exceptional, and a return of high unemployment in peacetime was still feared. The Coalition Government, therefore, made 'full employment' an essential part of its reconstruction policy. Plans were issued in 1944 which showed how drastically government thinking had changed on this subject. Expenditure on public works would be *encouraged* at any threat of depression—the opposite of the National Government's policy of economy in 1931. It was now realised that recovery from a depression was seriously hindered by the existence of mass unemployment.

As things turned out, the unemployment level after the war was even lower than the planners had hoped. Beveridge had assumed an average rate of eight per cent in his Report, but, in fact, it remained below two per cent! The conditions of world trade were largely responsible for this, but postwar governments were certainly more active in controlling industry than ever before. Much of the prosperity of the 1950s and 60s was based upon the successful curbing of unemployment. This, together with higher wages, helped to blunt the edge of much of the expected distress that National Insurance was designed to prevent. However in the 1970s rising unemployment again began to put a strain on the system of social security. The number of unemployed rose above a million, for the first time since the war, briefly in 1972 and for an extended period after 1974.

13 Health and Housing

The attack on the two remaining 'giants'—Disease and Squalor—was the special task of Aneurin Bevan, who, as Minister of Health, 1945–50, was responsible for both health and housing policy. The creation of a free health service was his personal ambition. His father had been a founder member of the Working Men's Medical Aid Society in Tredegar, Monmouthshire, and, in his earlier life, Aneurin Bevan had

Aneurin Bevan—at the Ministry of Health, 1945

seen ill health and squalor in abundance. Now was his chance to sweep it all away. The National Health Service, his greatest task, probably captured the imagination of the public more than any other reform of these years. It came into operation on the same day as National Insurance and National Assistance—5 July 1948.

'*The Appointed Day*'

On the evening of Sunday, 4 July 1948, Mr Attlee spoke to the nation on the B.B.C. Home Service. The subject of his broadcast was the official beginning of the Welfare State on the following day. The public was already well informed about the new services—largely as a result of a stream of explanatory leaflets and family guides. The Prime Minister could therefore concentrate on matters of wider importance. He was particularly anxious to stress the all-party origins of the social services; rightly refusing to take all the credit for his own party. Lloyd George and Beveridge, who had prepared so much of the ground, were Liberals, and most of the reconstruction plans had been made under a Conservative, Winston Churchill, while leader of a Coalition Government.

Mr Attlee explained that the quality of the new services would depend largely on the amount of money the country could afford to spend on them. It was therefore up to everyone to work hard to increase the national income, for 'the general level of production settles our standard of material well-being'. The national finances had not yet recovered from the war, and there were some, like the writer of a *Daily Mail*

editorial, who advised a postponement of some of the Government's plans until the country was back on its feet. But most people would not hear of any delay. The *Daily Mirror* summed up their feelings on 5 July:

'THE DAY IS HERE! For years the reformers of all parties have tried to safeguard the aged, the poor and the sick. Much has been done—much more than in any other large country. But always YOU wanted fuller protection against misfortune. You wanted the State to accept larger responsibility for the individual citizen who served it faithfully. YOU WANTED SOCIAL SECURITY. FROM THIS DAY HENCE, YOU HAVE IT.'

The National Health Service in the making

Like the other main services of the Welfare State which began their active life on the appointed day, the National Health Service was the result of wartime experience and planning. In 1939 the State health service was still basically that created by the Liberals in 1911. There had been growing public dissatisfaction with its shortcomings, especially the exclusion of the wives and children of insured workers from free medical treatment. The doctors themselves were not satisfied with 'Robin Hood medicine', which meant overcharging the rich in order to cover the cost of treating the poor free. Changes which had been contemplated for years without result were suddenly forced upon the Government by the war.

In 1938, fearing the outcome of German aggression in Europe, the Ministry of Health began to plan emergency medical services. Arrangements for the reception of air-raid casualties were especially important. To get some idea of what was needed, a survey was made of all hospital facilities—both municipal and voluntary. It revealed an overall shortage of hospital beds of about one-third—a desperate situation, considering the possibility of heavy war casualties! Many hospital buildings had been developed from Victorian workhouses. They had old-fashioned wards and equipment, in ugly, prisonlike buildings. To make matters worse there was a grave shortage of nursing staff. With no time to spare, the Government immediately set about providing additional beds, either in existing buildings or in special annexes and huts.

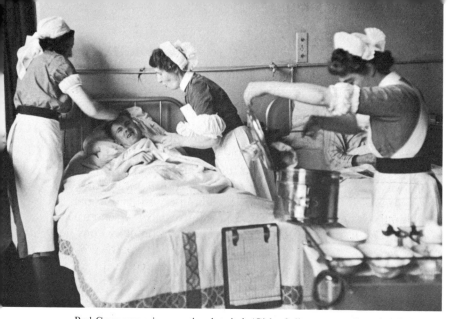

Red Cross nurses in a wartime hospital. (Girls of all ages entered nursing during the war to help relieve the staff shortage)

Equipment was also improved. Nearly 1,000 new operating theatres were installed by October 1939.

The supply of doctors and specialists also demanded urgent attention. They normally preferred to practise in pleasant, residential areas where most of the people were fairly well off. This was the best way of making sure they got their bills paid. Industrial towns, particularly in the depressed areas, were hardly attractive to doctors, with their high proportion of poor patients. There were seven times more doctors per head of the population in Kensington, one of the more pleasant areas of London, than in South Shields, in the heart of the depressed north-east. In view of the emergency, however, the Government was forced to interfere and transfer some of the doctors and specialists from desirable districts to the 'undoctored areas'.

The practical experience of war preparations revealed the urgent need for a full-scale State health service for all. It also provided an opportunity for experimenting with different methods of achieving it. Early in 1944, the Coalition Government produced a plan for a National Health Service which would be 'free to all' and financed out of national taxation:

'Just as people are accustomed to look to public organisa-

tion for essential facilities like a clean and safe water supply . . .
so they should now be able to look for proper facilities for the
care of their personal health to a publicly organised service
available to all who want to use it.'

The National Health Service Act

Labour took over the Coalition Government's plan, making
some important changes in it, and the National Health
Service Act was passed in 1946. The whole range of medical
treatment, including the services of dentists and opticians,
was to be provided free to everyone. No one would be compelled to use the State services. Doctors and patients who
wished to continue with private practice were free to do so,
but the aim was to make the State service so attractive and
complete that all would want to use it.

The hospital services were completely remodelled. The
Coalition Government had not intended that they should be
taken over by the State, but Labour, true to its principle of
nationalisation, took all but the teaching hospitals into public
ownership, under the Ministry of Health. England and Wales
was divided into fourteen sections (now fifteen), each under a
Regional Hospital Board. Bevan had been strongly opposed to
voluntary hospitals. He said medical care should not have to
rely on charity—nurses should be looking after the sick not
selling flags. Nevertheless, the voluntary spirit was not entirely
lost in the new service. The National League of Hospital
Friends was soon busy helping patients with things like shopping, and raising money for extra items like television sets,
telephone trolleys and bed curtains, which Hospital Management Committees could not always afford.

A national system of general practitioners—G.P.s—was
provided. To ensure their even distribution over the whole
country, the Medical Practices Committee would draft new
applicants to the 'undoctored areas'. Both doctors and patients
would have a free choice. Patients could change their doctor
if they wished to, and doctors could refuse to take certain
patients on their lists. If people fell ill while away from home,
they could call in any National Health doctor. All this varied
little from prewar days, except, of course, that everyone was
now included and there were no bills to pay.

County and County Borough Councils would provide midwives, home nurses and health visitors, and were responsible for vaccination, immunisation and the provision of ambulances. These services had normally been provided before but they had not previously been compulsory. A completely new idea, stemming from the wartime plan, was the introduction of local authority 'Health Centres'. Here family doctors would work together, with the latest equipment, and would be able to call in the skills of the specialist when required. This would be a valuable advance, for, as a British Medical Association report

Health Centre in Bristol, 1955

admitted 'the days when a doctor, armed only with his stethoscope and his drugs, could offer a fairly complete medical service are gone'.

The National Health Service Act was one of the most ambitious measures in parliamentary history—and one of the most successful. Yet it was nearly wrecked by the violent opposition of the doctors! Two months before the appointed day, two out of every three doctors voted against joining the service! They did not oppose the *principle* of a free health service for all, but they objected strongly to some of the details of the Act. They feared that the Government was trying to restrict their freedom and make them salaried civil servants, and they wanted a share in organising the services themselves. Bevan refused to give way on the major issues, although he did make some minor concessions to the doctors' demands—over things like the way they would be paid by the State. An uneasy truce was established, just in time for the service to begin as planned, but the argument between the doctors and the Government flared up again in 1964, due to a dispute over pay and conditions of work. Ever since Lloyd George's scheme of 1911, doctors have been very sensitive to State control and ready to assert their rights whenever they felt the Government was trying to restrict their freedom and responsibility.

The Stampede

'One would think the people saved up their illnesses for the first free day.' The comment of one G.P. probably summed up the feelings of thousands of others in the first few days of the National Health Service. Surgeries were invaded like bargain sales. The 'family doctor' service, so long out of reach of many people, was at last a reality for everyone, and they rushed to make use of it. Dentists came in for their share of attention. They were soon booked solid many months ahead, and there was even a five months wait for spectacles. Before long, Bevan had to make a special appeal to the public to use the National Health Service sensibly.

This was immediately seized upon by the critics of the scheme. They said the health service was merely an encouragement to people who wanted something for nothing and that the taxpayers' money was being needlessly squandered. However, the Government was quick to point out that much of the pressure on the health service resulted from prewar neglect. In 1939, for example, about 6 million people needed spectacles but did not have them. It was common practice for people to test their eyes in Woolworths and buy a pair of glasses for sixpence. The nation's teeth were also suffering from neglect. Local authority clinics found that most women had half or more of their teeth decayed or gone completely. Small wonder,

Typical waiting room

said the Government, that there was such a stampede for the services of National Health.

In any case, the scheme was not being run for the benefit of the poor alone. Most of the middle classes were very grateful for it too. Medical care had recently become very expensive for everyone. A G.P. commented: 'The local aristocracy have joined the National Health Service; they wait their turn in the surgery with the rest.' This was just what Bevan had hoped for. As he said, when the scheme started, 'we want everyone in, from the millionaires to the poorest'. Although this was not fully achieved, and some private practice continued, well over ninety-five per cent of all doctors and patients joined the State scheme. Only 6,000 'pay beds' were needed for private hospital patients, out of a total of over 240,000 beds.

In terms of money and manpower, the National Health Service became the second largest undertaking in the country —next to the armed forces. Nevertheless, there were still acute shortages of money and staff. Health centres, which were intended to be the heart of the health service, were still rare twenty years after the Act was passed. The first one was not

Mothers with babies wait to see the doctor at a mobile health centre—Ruislip, Middlesex, 1953

opened until 1952, at Woodberry Down, North London. Five years later, there were still less than twenty at work. Without health centres, the hospitals had to take on an increasing burden, and the queues of outpatients got longer and longer. The hospital building programme also suffered from lack of money. Hundreds of dreary, old-fashioned buildings still had to be used.

The great pressure on the National Health Service, and the vast expenditure which resulted, soon led to the introduction of charges on some of the services. Part of the cost of dentures had to be paid, and £1 was charged for each course of dental treatment for those over twenty-one. Prescription charges, and a contribution towards the cost of spectacles, were also added, although schoolchildren could still get free spectacles if they had standard frames. Bevan, then Minister of Labour, resigned from the Government in 1951 as a protest against these charges. He said they were against the principles of a *free* health service. With him went Harold Wilson, who, thirteen years later, as Prime Minister, had the satisfaction of seeing the prescription charge removed. Immediately, the number of prescriptions being issued rose sharply and the Conservative Opposition urged the Government to re-impose the charge.[1]

The problem of housing

In 1945 the housing situation was desperate. For six years building had almost ceased, while in the same period nearly one house in every three was damaged or destroyed by bombing. Even without war damage, more than 500,000 new houses were needed just to replace the worst slums. This was the size of the problem facing the Government, and Aneurin Bevan in particular, for until the formation of the Ministry of Housing and Local Government (1951) housing was the

" Well, were you or were you NOT the young couple advertising for a roof to put over their heads ? "

responsibility of the Minister of Health. An emergency housing drive was essential, but, before this could begin, temporary accommodation had to be found for the homeless. Aircraft

[1] Which they did in 1968, at the rate of 2s 6d.

factories were turned into prefabricated dwellings, and whole colonies of new 'prefabs' were built—a continuation of the Coalition Government's policy. Even then, many small houses had two families living in them.

Bevan concentrated on building subsidised council houses for renting. Private building for sale could only be carried on under licence and was severely restricted. This ensured that most of the resources of the building industry were concentrated on the Government's housing drive. Bevan was not satisfied with second-rate houses, thrown up in a hurry. Despite the emergency, he insisted that council houses should be good ones, with a natural life of about eighty years. They were expensive, but he refused to reduce standards. Even though materials were in short supply, Britain produced more new houses in the first five years after the war than any other European country.

The Government was accused of favouring the working class in its housing policy, but their needs were certainly the greatest immediately after the war. Gradually, as the shortage was reduced, council housing became more classless, like the other social services. A Housing Act of 1949 showed this change of attitude. Local authorities were to provide for *all*, not just the 'working class'. By the 1950s a wide cross-section of society occupied council houses, many of them with well-paid jobs and expensive cars. People who had been used to thinking of council houses as a special service for the poor objected to this. They said it was unfair to give subsidised houses to people who could afford to pay the full rent. There has been much debate on this issue ever since. It is by no means generally accepted that housing should be a social service for all, in the same way as school milk or medical care.

In the ten years after the war, three-quarters of all new houses had been built by local authorities. A quarter of the total population now lived in publicly owned property. Although the housing shortage still seemed never-ending, great progress had been made. An Act of 1956 discontinued all government subsidies to local authorities, except those for slum clearance and the building of new towns. From then on, private house-building accelerated once more. An increasing number of people began to borrow money from building societies and buy their own houses—although prices were too high for house purchase to be possible for lower-paid workers, especially in London and the south-east.

New and expanding towns

The New Towns Act (1946) combined the need to build more houses with the task of reducing overcrowding in the great cities. New communities were to be established close to London and other big cities to take their 'overspill'. The land would be bought by compulsory purchase, and local authorities would receive government subsidies to help them build houses for renting. The first twelve new towns were planned by 1950.

Blocks of flats going up and already occupied, Harlow New Town, Essex—1951

In the next twenty-five years, twenty more were planned and started—bringing the total to twenty-two in England and Wales, five in Scotland and four in Northern Ireland. By then (1975) new towns housed nearly 2 million people. They have many attractive features. Work and residence can be brought closer together, and planners are given opportunities to put new ideas into practice. Things like traffic-free shopping centres, the separation of the industrial zone from the residential areas and

The new towns of Britain (excluding N. Ireland) in 1970

improved traffic control are easier to achieve in a town which is carefully planned as a whole before a brick is laid.

Another experiment which proved very successful was the subject of the Town Development Act, 1952. The Government decided to assist the expansion of existing small towns which were willing to take some of the population from overcrowded cities. Worsley, in Lancashire, had already begun to take the overspill from nearby Salford before the Act was passed, and Wolverhampton and Walsall had made similar arrangements before 1952. Bletchley, Aylesbury and Swindon soon followed, and a number of other 'expanded towns' were planned for the future.

Although housing remains one of Britain's greatest problems, many of the worst evils have been overcome. A large number of 'condemned' houses are still standing, and the overall shortage appears to be permanent, but it is no longer possible to speak of housing in terms of the 'giant Squalor'.

14 Poverty and the Welfare State in York, 1950

All the separate parts of the Welfare State had been fitted into place by 1948. Soon afterwards, Seebohm Rowntree completed his series of investigations into poverty in York. He was, naturally, concerned above all with one important question: '... how far the various welfare measures which have come into force since 1936 (the date of the previous survey) have succeeded in reducing poverty'. It is an appropriate question on which to end our own study of the making of the Welfare State. By confining our attention to York, we can once more get a close-up view of what the social services really meant in the lives of ordinary people.

Poverty and the social services

As before, Rowntree began by calculating a 'poverty line'. In addition to food, clothing and necessary household expenditure like fuel and lighting, he added a small allowance for 'personal sundries'—travel, wireless licence, newspapers, postage, stationery and so on. By 1950 the standard of living had risen so much that it was unrealistic to leave these things out. In fact, things like drink and cigarettes were rarely cut out altogether in times of hardship. They were merely reduced and some more essential items were cut down as well. For this reason, it was always difficult to draw a satisfactory poverty line; people rarely spent all their money sensibly. Nevertheless, leaving out rent and rates, Rowntree estimated that £5 0s 2d was the minimum weekly income necessary for a family of five. This was again adjusted to fit all family sizes, including single people living alone.

Instead of interviewing every working-class family in a population of 105,000, Rowntree arranged to have a sample taken of one house in nine where the main income of the family was below £10 10s 0d. This 'sample method' was satisfactorily used in all kinds of social investigations by this time. On the basis of this research, Rowntree calculated that 1,746 persons were living in poverty—only 1·6 per cent of the whole population. We are now in a position to summarise half a century of social progress in one simple table, but, before we do so, there are two important things to remember. First, these figures are only for 'primary poverty'. In other words, they take no account of people who had enough income but got themselves into poverty by spending some of it unwisely. Second, the 1950 figure would be lower if it was based on the same standard of living as the other two. The 1950 poverty line was a good deal more generous than those of 1899 and 1936.

THE REDUCTION OF POVERTY, 1899–1950

	1899	1936	1950
Percentage of the total population in poverty	9·9	3·9	1·6
Main cause of poverty	Low wages	Unemployment	Old age

As you can see from the table, old age had become the main cause of poverty by 1950. In fact, it accounted for more than two-thirds of the total. Obviously the retirement pension was still far too low. Many of these old people were receiving supplementary pensions as well, yet they still could not manage. Some cases of hardship found among pensioners were more typical of the 'bad old days' than the mid-twentieth century. An old man of seventy-six said he had no money for replacement of any household goods or clothes. His sole pleasure, an ounce of tobacco a week, had to be given up for several weeks when he had his shoes repaired. Another pensioner said: 'These clothes will have to last until I die; I shall never be able to afford any more.' Nevertheless, even though in poverty, many expressed deep gratitude for the new scheme of social security. Before 1948 most of them had lived on less. If the Welfare State had not abolished poverty altogether, it had at least reduced its amount and severity.

Perhaps the most remarkable discovery in the whole survey was the fact that not a single family was in poverty through unemployment. The reason for this was not that National Insurance benefits were sufficient on their own, although they were much more substantial than they had ever been, but that the few who were out of work had some form of extra income in addition to unemployment benefit. The high level of employment which had been maintained since the war had obviously played a great part in reducing poverty. Rowntree was sure that if mass unemployment returned, on the scale of the 1930s, it would have a marked effect on the numbers in poverty. He calculated that if 8·8 per cent of workmen had been unemployed (which had been the figure in York in 1936) poverty would have more than doubled.

Rowntree made another interesting calculation. He applied the welfare services in force in 1936 to the situation in 1950, in an attempt to estimate the extent to which the most recent reforms were responsible for the reduction in poverty. He could not give a complete picture, because many of the benefits of the Welfare State could not be measured in figures. Therefore no account was taken of things like the National Health Service or housing subsidies. His final estimate was that the 1950 poverty figure would have increased by about eight times if the Welfare State had been in its 1936 stage of development. However, these figures are extremely unreliable and open to much criticism. They could not take account of things like changes in taxation and the general standard of living.

Housing and health

By 1950, four-fifths of all houses in York were classed as 'satisfactory'. The other fifth were planned for demolition by 1967. Overcrowding had virtually disappeared. The only serious black mark remaining was the absence of bathrooms in almost half of the houses occupied by workmen. Considering the effect of six years of war on the housing programme, York City Council had made great progress since 1936. Well over a fifth of all the houses in the city were council houses. The subsidies on them were an important part of the benefits of the Welfare State. Rowntree concluded: 'We do not suggest that . . . everybody now has adequate accommodation, on the contrary, many rooms are dark and small, particularly in the

New flats in York, opened 1951 by the Duchess of Gloucester

houses scheduled for demolition. . . . But the fact remains that substantial progress has been made since 1936.'

It was not possible to form any exact estimate of the value of the National Health Service. Most of its benefits could not be measured—although there could be no doubt that most people had gained tremendously from the wide range of medical services now freely available to them. Some idea of the general improvement in physique can be got from the fact that children of all ages were taller and heavier than they had been in 1936.

AVERAGE HEIGHTS AND WEIGHTS OF SCHOOLCHILDREN, 1936–50

		Average Weight	Average Height
Children from families *just above* the poverty line	1936	67 lb	52 inches
	1950	69½ lb	52¼ inches
Children from families wealthy enough to send them to a private school (i.e. 'middle class')	1936	74½ lb	53¾ inches
	1950	76 lb	54¼ inches

This trend has continued ever since, as the nation gets healthier. The most important reason for the improvement in the physique of children was undoubtedly the great expansion of maternity and infant welfare services since the outbreak of the war.

The task not yet complete

This third survey of York was published in 1951—the year of Rowntree's eightieth birthday, and three years before his death. He could look back on a lifetime which had spanned the most remarkable social progress in the entire history of Britain. The York of 1899 had changed out of all recognition. The Welfare State had arrived and appeared to be working, but, as Rowntree pointed out, it was still far from perfect. The great reduction in poverty was not entirely due to the social services. More women than ever were working in 1950, and their extra income often made the difference between poverty and a comfortable standard of living. Also, the survey was carried out at a time when there was virtually no unemployment. Without these two factors, York in 1950 would have presented a very different picture.

There was, after all, still hardship. The problem of poverty had become very largely the problem of old age. Pensions had never been sufficient in the first place, but they were now falling rapidly behind the cost of living. With the proportion of elderly people in the community increasing yearly, this was a grave problem. Many old people were too proud to go to the National Assistance Board and ask for what they regarded as charity. After the survey was completed, in the budget of 1951, pensions were increased. Rowntree calculated that if this had been done before his investigation it would have halved his figure for the total numbers in poverty. This shows how necessary the increase was, and how important it would be in the future to keep pension rates in line with changes in the cost of living.

15 Conclusion

The Welfare State, as it stands today, was created between 1940 and 1948—but its roots are deep in the past. The burst of activity in the 1940s was the climax to more than a century of social reform—a century during which the State took on ever-increasing responsibility for the welfare of the whole community. Nevertheless, though firmly based on past experience, the remarkable social progress of the period 1940–48 will always stand apart in British history. For the first time, social services were planned and created as part of an overall scheme. Each of Beveridge's 'five giants' was vigorously attacked, with great success.

The Second World War was a decisive influence on social policy, coming as it did after a period of distress and hardship in many parts of Britain. It drew together the whole community in face of a common danger and kindled a new spirit of comradeship, and a desire to banish long-standing social evils. As Beveridge said in his Report: 'War breeds national unity. It may be possible, through a sense of national unity . . . to bring about changes which . . . it might be difficult to make at other times.'

Social security or Santa Claus?

Now that the wartime spirit of social improvement has passed, and memories of 'dole' queues and the means test are fading, it is easy for us to take the Welfare State for granted. Nowadays we *expect* the Government to look after our interests —to educate us, provide medical care when we are sick and financial security in time of need. Yet we rarely stop to think how all these things are paid for. We grumble freely at increased taxes, while National Insurance contributions are thought of merely as something which reduces 'take home pay'.

On the morning of 'Appointed Day', 5 July 1948, *The Times* asked: 'Can the next generation reap the benefits of a social service State while avoiding the perils of a Santa Claus State?' Many members of the older generation would say that the 'perils' have *not* been avoided. They would very likely claim that today people 'have it too easy', and that having everything 'served up on a plate' takes away initiative and ambition. The *Punch* cartoon is a good example of the kind of criticism that has been made of the Welfare State since it began. It dates from 1949, but it could have been drawn yesterday.

THE WELFARE STATE

However, many critics appear to be missing the point. Neither Beveridge nor the Government intended the State to become a kind of hammock on which people could doze peacefully, free from care. The object of the Beveridge Report was 'not that of a Welfare State providing everything that the citizen could desire. The idea was that of a minimum guaranteed by the State.' It was assumed that the individual would use his abilities to the full to secure 'something above the minimum'. In this way, ambition and drive would still be essential to secure a good standard of living.

No doubt some people *have* sat back and been content with second best, secure in the knowledge that they would be provided for in the last resort. But the vast majority have responded to the Welfare State in the way Beveridge hoped they would. There is no real evidence that people today are less energetic or ambitious than their parents were.

An American critic once said to Beveridge that if there had been social security in the days of Elizabeth I there would probably have been no Drake, Hawkins or Raleigh. Beveridge replied that *these* great Elizabethans had had social security from birth: 'Adventure came not from the half-starved, but from those who were well-fed enough to feel ambition.' In the sixteenth century, 'freedom from want' was the privilege of a small section of society—as it was even 300 years later, in Victoria's reign. Beveridge, and all those who put his ideas into practice, wanted this freedom extended to every citizen as a birthright. It has now very largely been achieved, and the 'War on Want' has been carried overseas—to the under-developed countries of Africa and Asia. In modern Britain, and in most other Western societies—which have undergone similar 'social revolutions'—rich and poor are now very small minorities. And differences in living standards between the middle and lower classes are less clear-cut than they used to be. Never before have the pleasures of life and the benefits of civilisation been available to so many people.

'Casualties of the Welfare State'

In opposition to those who say the Welfare State makes life too easy for people, there are many critics who think it does not go far enough. They point to the large number of 'casualties'—people in need who find that the State does *not* in fact provide a reasonable minimum standard of living. National Insurance benefits alone have never been enough to live on for any length of time—although the introduction of wage-related benefits (1966) was certainly an important step forward. Of course, this has not been a problem for most people of working age because, since the war, high wages and full employment have helped to raise the standard of living even more than was hoped. But many *old people* have suffered greatly from the failure to fix adequate minimum rates of benefit. This is the greatest problem of the Welfare State, because soon there will be more bath-chairs than prams in the community.

Unless they have other means, like a private pension or savings, the aged need to apply for a Supplementary (extra) Pension. However, many of them refuse to do this, preferring to remain in poverty and keep their 'self respect'. The memory of the poor law lingers on. In 1963, while $2\frac{1}{2}$ million people were being supported by the National Assistance Board, a further million were entitled to assistance but did not apply for it. This was an important reason for the scrapping of the National Assistance Board and the setting up of the unified Ministry of Social Security (1966). It enabled enquiries about the entire range of social security benefits to be dealt with at one point of contact. Those who may have been reluctant to advertise their poverty by going to the old National Assistance Board are now more likely to claim in full the allowances they are entitled to.

As well as old people, *large families* can often be 'casualties of the Welfare State'—especially as family allowances have lagged far behind rises in the cost of living. To help the poorest parents, a Family Income Supplement scheme (F.I.S.) was started in 1971. Low-paid workers with children are entitled to claim weekly allowances on top of their wages, the amount depending on their income and the size of their family. Those receiving F.I.S. can also claim free school meals for their children; free prescriptions, dental treatment and glasses under the National Health, and various other benefits in-cluding free welfare milk for children under five. But some or all of these benefits can be lost if the head of the family gets a wage rise taking him above F.I.S. levels. So the scheme gives the lowly-paid little incentive to increase their earnings. Its critics have called it a 'poverty trap', and pointed out similarities with the Speenhamland System of the eighteenth century (see p. 8).

Lack of money has prevented many of the ambitious schemes of 1942–48 from being realised. Modern, fully-equipped health centres are still the exception rather than the rule. The idea of part-time education in county colleges for all early school leavers has been forgotten. Shortages of staff and equipment continue to hamper the Health Service, while many hospitals, schools and old people's homes carry on in outdated buildings. The housing shortage seems to have become permanent.

So in many respects the bright hopes of the 1940s have not been fulfilled. Those who say that the Welfare State does not go far enough appear to have a strong case.

Pointers for the future

All political parties agree on the desirability of re-shaping the social services. And already they have begun to move away from Beveridge's principle of *universal* services (available to all, regardless of income) to *selective* services (concentrated on those who have the greatest financial need). Looking to the future, perhaps the most urgent need is to provide greater assistance for old people and large families on low incomes. But there is also grave concern about oversized school classes, council house waiting lists and the difficulty of maintaining standards of medical care. Whether the State can afford necessary improvements will depend upon the national income, which, in turn, depends upon the level of productivity from those at work. As Clement Attlee said on the eve of Appointed Day: 'The general level of production settles our standard of material well-being.'

Important changes have already taken place in the system of social security. The idea of wage-related benefits, introduced in 1966, was taken a stage further in 1975 when a new Earnings Related Scheme came into operation. The familiar stamp card was abolished for all 'employed earners' and National Insurance contributions became wholly related to earnings, calculated as a percentage of gross pay. For the bulk of the working population, the rate of contribution was set at 5.5 per cent of all earnings up to a certain limit (£69 per week in 1975). Above the limit no further contributions were required. The benefits payable under the new scheme were based on contributions, so that the better-off paid more and got more in return. In this way social security benefits were related to the normal wage-earning capacity of each individual more closely than ever before.

Timeline

Milestones in the making of the Welfare State

1834   Poor Law Amendment Act—workhouses for the 'able-bodied poor'

1848   First Public Health Act

1850   Factory Act—ten-and-a-half-hour day

1870   Elementary Education Act—beginning of Board Schools

1875   Artisans' Dwellings Act—to promote slum clearance

1880   Compulsory education

1883   Diseases Prevention Act—non-poor law hospitals

1890   Housing of the Working Classes Act

1891   Free elementary education

1897   Workmen's Compensation Act

1902   Education Act—Local Education Authorities and State secondary education

1905   Unemployed Workmen Act

1906   School meals for poor children

1907   School medical inspection
        Scholarships to secondary schools—'free places'

1908   Children Act—protection of children, Juvenile Courts, probation service
        Old Age Pensions—non-contributory

1909   'The People's Budget'—graduated taxation
        Trade Boards—for fixing wages in 'sweated industries'
        Labour exchanges

1911   National Insurance Act—insurance against sickness and unemployment

1918   Education Act—leaving age fixed at fourteen

1919 ⎫
1923 ⎬ Subsidised Housing Acts—local authority 'council houses'
1924 ⎭

1920   Unemployment insurance extended to most workers
-21   and their dependants

1925 Contributory Old Age, Widows' and Orphans' Pensions

1926 Hadow Report—recommended State secondary education for all

1929 Local Government Act—abolished Poor Law Unions and Guardians of 1834

1931 'Means test'

1934 Milk Act
Unemployment Assistance Board—for long-term unemployed

1940 School milk and meals for all
–41 National Milk Scheme and vitamin foods for young children
Unemployment Assistance Board becomes Assistance Board
Supplementary pensions

1942 Beveridge Report on Social Insurance

1944 Education Act—secondary education for all

1945 Family Allowances Act

1946 National Health Service Act
New Towns Act
National Insurance Act; Industrial Injuries Insurance Act

1948 '*Appointed Day*', *5 July*—official beginning of the Welfare State
National Assistance Board
Children Act

1952 Town Development (Expanding Towns) Act

1961 Graduated Retirement Pensions

1966 Wage-related Short-term Benefits

1968 Department of Health and Social Security

1971 Family Income Supplements

1975 Earnings Related Benefits

Further Reading
and Research

You can get a good idea of what life was like before the Welfare State from the works of novelists. These are particularly relevant:

DICKENS, CHARLES. *Oliver Twist*, illustrated by Ronald Searle. Longmans.
— *David Copperfield*, any edition.
— *Nicholas Nickleby*, any edition.
GASKELL, ELIZABETH. *Mary Barton*, any edition.
LONDON, JACK. *The People of the Abyss*. ARCO (Fitzroy edition).
ORWELL, GEORGE. *Down and Out in Paris and London* (Second part). Gollancz; Penguin.
— *Road to Wigan Pier*. Penguin.
GREENWOOD, WALTER. *Love on the Dole*. Cape.

The following, written specially for young people, should be helpful for reference:

LINDSAY, D., and WASHINGTON, E. S. *A Portrait of Britain, 1851–1951*. O.U.P. (especially chapter 22).
SPEED, P. F. *Learning and Teaching in Victorian Times*. Longmans (Then and There Series).
WHITTAKER, D. *The Social Services*. Longman (Social Science Studies series).
MARSH, J. *The Welfare State*. Harrap (New Generation series).
SCHOOLS COUNCIL/NUFFIELD HUMANITIES PROJECT: *Poverty*. Heinemann (a pack of source materials, plus tapes and slides).

Research

There is very little that is suitable written on the period after 1940. The best way of finding out about recent developments in the social services is to do some private research. There are three good ways of going about it:

1. RELATIONS AND FRIENDS OF THE FAMILY

Ask older members of your family, and their friends, about life in Britain before and after the Welfare State was created. If you have any grandparents living near you, put them at the top of your list.

They will probably be delighted to tell you about their early lives, and they are sure to be impressed by your knowledge and interest. Ask them about their schooldays, and about the social services when they first started work. Get them to tell you about the years of depression and the Second World War. Your parents will explain how the present-day social services work. They have seen them develop since the 1940s, and they will remember people like Beveridge, Bevan, Churchill and Attlee.

2. GOVERNMENT OFFICES

There may well have been some changes in the social services since this book was published. For really up-to-date information, you should consult your local offices of the Department of Health and Social Security. There you will be able to obtain printed pamphlets giving the present rates of benefits, and details of any new schemes that have been, or are about to be, introduced.

3. PUBLIC LIBRARIES

Your local public library will have a reference section, containing books and periodicals which cannot be taken away. The library staff are specially trained to help you find out things for yourself. They will offer advice on the best way of finding out more about the social services in your locality—both past and present. If you live in a large town, the reference section of the main library may have a special local history department. Here you can trace the local results of the developments which have been described on a nationwide scale in this book.

Index